D1237232

Culture / Flesh

Social Philosophy Research Institute Book Series

Culture / Flesh

Explorations of Postcivilized Modernity

Michael A. Weinstein

Social Philosophy Research Institute
Book Series

ROWMAN & LITTLEFIELD PUBLISHERS, INC.

ROWMAN & LITTLEFIELD PUBLISHERS, INC.

Published in the United States of America
by Rowman & Littlefield Publishers, Inc.
4720 Boston Way, Lanham, Maryland 20706

3 Henrietta Street
London WC2E 8LU, England

British Cataloging in Publication Information Available

Library of Congress Cataloging-in-Publication Data
Weinstein, Michael A.
Culture/flesh : explorations of postcivilized modernity / Michael
A. Weinstein,
p.   cm.—(Social Philosophy Research Institute book series)
Includes index.
1. Man.   2. Postmodernism.   3. Civilization, Modern—20th century.
4. Culture.   5. Sex.   I. Title.   II. Series.
BD450.W44   1995 128—dc20   95-8964   CIP
ISBN 0-8476-8083-5 (cloth: alk. paper)
ISBN 0-8476-8084-3 (pbk.: alk. paper)

Printed in the United States of America

 ^{TM} The paper used in this publication meets the minimum requirements of
American National Standard for Information Sciences-Permanence of
Paper for Printed Library Materials, ANSI Z39.48–1984.

Contents

Preface

The postcivilized modern condition is marked by a sharp contradiction between culture and flesh. Human beings worship their products. Their products penetrate and transform their flesh. The human flesh becomes a sacrifice to the human product. The flesh rebels.

The postcivilized modernist is the rebel of the flesh in and against the so-called postmodern condition. He says that the struggle is not over yet, that language does not yet ''speak him.'' The modern individual has not vanished but now knows that he is what he has always been: a sentient and self-aware organism (the flesh) who fights a losing battle against adversity. To be a postcivilized modernist means to admit that the modern myths of man, progress, reason, and nature were simply symbolic compensations for the failure of finite life. With demystification the failure of life becomes clear and conscious, its weakness revealed by the tyranny over it of its own product, culture.

The grand project of modern civilization was to transform nature through the means of technology into a fit habitation for man, to ''humanize'' the world. That project is over. The world has been humanized, but it is not a fit habitation for human beings. Rather, a second nature, culture, has been thrown over the first one and is no less adverse to the flesh than the one it was supposed to perfect. Culture has become an environment, a jungle for restless monkeys that penetrates to their inwardness. It is as objective as nature. Culture does not belong to ''man,'' who has vanished. It surely does not belong to those who may believe that they own it, that it is their expression or utensil, but who mainly worship it. Culture is now free from being controlled by its producers. Yet it can be appropriated and reappropriated endlessly by them.

Enter the civil savage, the postcivilized modernist as survivor and sometimes prevailer in the culture jungle, the love pirate, the devoted appropriator. My viewpoint is masculine and the savage is male—a frame of reference I will explain later.

This is the book of the civil savage, who seeks to live well in the culture jungle. As a civil savage, I accede to the judgment that modern civilization is a dead letter, that its mythic unities are no longer credible. I share with postmodernists the judgment that culture has become a great independent power, but not so great that the centered self has necessarily been deconstructed or demonstrated to be a grammatical fiction. I choose to deploy an ego-centered discourse (even postmodernists allow that), but I also believe, as postmodernists usually do not, that my discourse is referential, that it expresses my judgments, which are the judgments of self-aware, imagining, and feeling flesh, of a center of finite life grasped consciously from the inside. It is true, however, that my judgments are expressed in language, which, as culture, is not mine unless I transform it from a social product into an organ for expressing conscious and feeling flesh. As I make that transformation I bring forth my centered self, which is irredeemably coconstituted by the language I use. There is no self apart from language, but language can contribute to defining a self that uses language to express self-understandings and valuations of its circumstances. The postcivilized modernist is the modernist inventing a life in the so-called postmodern condition. The civil savage is a demystified modernist set loose on the postmodern scene, claiming that his "subject position" is not merely a mystification.

The civil savage's discourse, my discourse, is a free meditation concerned with how to come to terms with what Max Weber termed "the disenchantment of the world," which for me means the reduction of the self to the finite flesh and the advent of culture as a second nature. The flesh is weak and ever prone to worship. Now, lacking anything transcendent in which to ground itself, it tends to worship its own products at the expense of itself, an ultimate irony. Rebelling against culture worship, the civil savage takes the way of strengthening the finite individual in order to make the individual fit to enjoy the pleasures that are provided by the world, not the pleasures of self-absorbing fantasies that are generated in culture worship. The civil savage is a hedonist, but one who cherishes that which brings pleasure, not one who interprets and uses the other as a means to a private satisfaction. For the civil savage, pleasure is not an isolated sensation but a relationship that includes feeling as one of its components, along with activity that links self to other things and persons. His hedonism is erotic in the broad sense of seeking union with the pleasure-providing other, but the eroticism is respectful of difference and conscious of his limits and those of the other person or thing. Through the creation of a strong centric ego and the life strategy of erotic hedonism, the civil savage vindicates the finite flesh against its own temptations to humiliate itself. Anhedonia is the spiritual disease of postcivilized modernity. The civil savage offers a specific for it, a transvaluation of postmodernity asserting the privilege of flesh over culture.

Like the renegade in two of my previous free meditations, *The Tragic Sense of Political Life* and *The Structure of Human Life*, the civil savage is a philosophical persona, a personification of a way of engaging in circumstances and interpreting self that I invite readers to appreciate, criticize, and, above all, appropriate for their own uses. The renegade was defined by a refusal to attenuate or reverse the judgment that life is a losing proposition. The civil savage is still a renegade, but has moved beyond refusal by learning and becoming fit to love that which he can find or make lovable in his circumstances. Through that process the refusal has become softened by the embraces. The renegade and civil savage encapsulate an experiment in attempting to live well in deep connection with, rather than withdrawal from, the world, under the horizon of irredeemable death, disease, and decay of myself and loved ones, and played out in the culture jungle of postcivilized modernity.

The civil savage's discourse is written with many masculine pronouns. That is because it was composed as a male discourse in full awareness of feminist criticisms of the masculine mystique. It seemed most respectful of difference in this case to write as a man, even when I was writing about all individuals. I hope that civil savagery gives certain themes of traditionally male thinking, such as control and militancy, some new turns that bend them toward love rather than possessiveness and willfulness. Though it is a male discourse, my intent is to welcome female readers and invite them to plunder it for ways of strengthening their own survival and enjoyment of life. Indeed, one of the aims of the civil savage is to present a version of the masculine that is more accessible to female appropriation than previous male texts, parading in the guise of the human, or ''man'', have been. More importantly, regardless of pronouns, I make no distinction between women and men as discrete centers of finite conscious life. Yet that itself might be construed by some as a male idea.

I acknowledge and thank Dr. John Loughney for the great contribution that he made to this writing. He gave its first draft an exceedingly careful reading, pointing out with intelligence and sympathy the points at which I had deviated from my better self and had become dogmatic

and even perverse. The civil savage's discourse is far better intellectually and morally than it would have been without his intervention,
which was an act of fine intellectual friendship. As usual, I thank my
colleague Deena Weinstein for conversation, criticism, and constructive
reading.

Chapter 1

Civilization

It has become fashionable in recent years, at least among cultural critics, to discourse about a new global phenomenon in human history that is usually designated "postmodernity." In the following reflections I shall attempt to make a contribution to the discussions about a presumed new age, to define what has happened to the general structure of life in the West during the twentieth century, and to indicate how it might be possible to live well within the contemporary situation. I share with the proponents of postmodernism the conviction that individuals in the West encounter a genuinely novel condition of life, which is deeply disquieting and poses severe challenges to the will merely to continue living, not to speak of the desire to live well. However, I part with them on the matter of defining this condition, which appears not so much to be the passing of modernity as the passing of one of its aspects, civilization; that is, I question the easy identification implied by the term "modern civilization" and shall argue that the Western individual is now experiencing the phase of postcivilized modernity, a return to savagery within the environment or horizon of high technology.

The emergence of savagery amidst the ruins of civilization impels me to undertake a meditation on philosophy of conduct, if only to draw attention to the horizon of possibilities that individuals might entertain as they seek to hold on to their existence day by day, to survive and, perhaps, to flourish. In the present moment of Western history, life is being sustained by the remains of past civilization, just as a landscape might be illuminated by the light generated by a star that has already died. The current moment will not last very long, as habits of civilized thinking increasingly fall into disuse: work should begin to understand what civilization essentially is, how it has been dissipated, what might still be salvaged from it, and what might take its place.

The thesis that the West is passing through a postcivilized era has no claim to self-evidence and, therefore, can be supported only by an extended analysis, including interpretations of such terms as "civilization," "modernity," and "savagery." I shall undertake such an analysis in the form of a free meditation; that is, I will present with as much clarity as I can the ways in which I have achieved my thesis and have understood its consequences for the conduct of life. Using the medical analogy favored by Karl Mannheim, I shall offer a "diagnosis of the times" and some therapeutic suggestions. Just as good physicians do not confine themselves to particular methods and procedures but employ a wide variety of specialized and impressionistic means to understand and remediate their patients' ailments, I shall use logical analysis, public fact, historical observation, intuition, phenomenological description, introspection, common sense, insights from a variety of theories and ideologies, and results of the human sciences to clarify circumstance and possibility. I will not, generally, utilize these disparate forms of thinking within their own systematizations and strictly according to their own standards, but will attempt to weave them together, often in such a way that their specific strands are not apparent, into an invitation to experience life in the way that has become compelling to me. My appeal is to the kind of insight that sometimes appears in the best of free discussions, in which the participants assent to the cogency of one another's visions of things and to their ways of holding them. There is no single test for truth in such discussions, only the experience of grasping the seriousness and relevance of the other's intent, and the pertinence of their insight and evidence. Yet conversation does have a discipline, which allows it to take on a systematic character: thematic unity and appreciation of the other's integrity. I am writing to individuals, with respect for and acknowledgment of their differences from me, about the lives we lead.

I begin with a reflection on the romance of civilization, after which I will conduct a rapid tour of some of the great world civilizations (East Asian, Indian, Islamic, Athenian, Christian, and modern) with the intent of displaying what I have grasped to be their import for understanding and conducting individual life. Then, having exposed what in the past have been taken to be our truest and best possibilities, I will be ready to discuss our current plight. I call civilization a romance because I believe that at its root it responds to the deep human desire for a unity of being and goodness. "Being is good," the first principle of Thomas Aquinas's philosophy, is the foundation of every world civilization, the incentive and promise that civilization offers to the individual in return for the terrible sacrifice it exacts. Civilization requires the individual to stand alone, at least for some moments, apart from the continuous support of a communal mind that draws the separate self out of isolation and into a wider social experience, the round of everyday life. Civilization occurs in the spiritual act of removing the individual self from its connections to an ongoing community, revealing the self to itself as a strange and fragile being, and then reconnecting the self to a reality surpassing in its being and goodness the reality of the particular community. From that vision of a profounder reality, the individual returns to everyday life with a new way of relating to community, as a self that constitutes community, along with others, out of inward direction.

I offer my dialectical romance of immersion in dreamlike unity, estrangement and disclosure of individual being, reunion through self-transcendence, and unification with others through self-conscious apprehension of the goodness of being, as the structure of the world religions and of the civilizations that they reflectively expressed and, therefore, informed or impressed with form. Civilization, in this view, is founded on the crucial moment in which the self discovers that there is a reality, transcending the habit, custom, ritual, and myth of the community, which is also good-in-itself and worthy of being affirmed or, more accurately, which compels affirmation. That is the "good news," which varies from one civilization to the next, according to the way in which what Pitirim Sorokin called the "reality-truth-value" was grasped. However, there is a counterpoint to the dominant theme that being is good, which is the fragile, torn, and humbled (if not humiliated) self, caught in the moment between the dissolution of communal ties and the regrounding in transcendence. This is another truth, which is constant in all civilizations and which they must acknowledge and then sublimate by denying its finality. Each civilization is a way or ways to achieve this sublimation, to reach the conviction that being is good. To be postcivilized is to find all the ways blocked: No exit.

The term "civilization," as I shall use it here, refers fundamentally and essentially to a dialectical process of consciousness or, better, of spirituality in a broad Hegelian sense, in which human existence comes to be grounded in an inwardly grasped apprehension of being, an apprehension removed from the specifications of social convention. Thus, the core of civilization, from which all of the many works associated with it spring, is self-concentration, the seizure of individuality that provides

the self with a criterion of judgment transcending custom and arti-
fice, and compacting aesthetic, cognitive, and volitional dimensions
of mentality into an integral strategy of relating self to other. This
understanding of civilization is radically aristocratic, in the sense of
José Ortega y Gasset, drawing upon the documents of elite culture and
attempting to relive the spiritual journeys that they recount. The civilized mind is constituted by what Max Scheler called a "unit experience," which is a complex integrity, readily identifiable as a phenomenon when it appears. This experience of separation, union, and
reunification is, in the language of Edmund Husserl's phenomenology,
the "essence" of civilization, which is diversified in each world civilization according to the object of union. I do not, then, derive my romance of civilization from a generalization based on historical or empirical observation, but from insight into a singular structure of mind,
which I am compelled to acknowledge each time I study the documents
that are generally identified as the guiding texts of the world civilizations. There is a circle involved in my method and reasoning, but it is
not vicious, it is merely a variant of the familiar hermeneutical circle:
inquirers must somehow know what they are looking for before they
find it.

In my case the documents of the world civilizations were alluring
because they promised to reveal knowledge that might make my life
coincident with itself, disclose myself to myself in my best possibilities.
So I studied them to seek the truth they might contain and then tried to
be as receptive as I could to that truth if, indeed, there was one, as a
concrete experience. Such a form of inquiry does not proceed in the
scientific way by deriving an hypothesis from theoretical propositions
and then testing it, but sets out from as few prepossessions as possible
and strains toward new insight. When that insight comes the circle is
broken: one knows that one has found something, even if there can be
no assurance that it is exactly the same thing as those who generated
the texts and those who have appropriated them as tradition intended.
There is genuine surprise involved in achieving fresh insight, wonder,
if you will, in Aristotle's sense, which does not eventuate directly in
public knowledge but which gives confidence and assurance through
the way in which it organizes the various aspects of life into an intelligible pattern.

I cannot prove, then, that I have reached an accurate understanding
of the world civilizations, that such an understanding can even be at-
tained, or that there is a single spiritual core informing each of them.
Each of my interpretations may reveal only my reading of my private
fantasy and, most deeply, my romance of civilization may be a master
fantasy, a kind of metapsychosis. Here is an indication of what it means

to be a postcivilized sophisticate, a learned savage who, at least in public, cannot wear his sagacity well, if, indeed, he has it. If I am correct, civilization is founded in an inward experience and, as a public affair, which it must be, is based on the assumption that inwardness can be transmitted symbolically to transform the inwardness of others. Yet I am living in a cultural world that is so dominated by science and technology, that privileges the externally perceptible so much, that I cannot discuss my subject without going on the defensive and making apologies. My doubts are not mere formalities. I have internalized the voices of the technological jungle, the complaints of the specialists who demand empirical verification in the social sciences and documentation in the humanities. If one ventures beyond the footnote, the census table, or the questionnaire, one is thrown into the sea of subjectivity, which means that one is abandoned to sink or swim with only the resources of one's own intellectual and spiritual character for support. For the specialist, nothing could be worse than that. In a society that privileges technology to the exclusion of nearly any other form of culture, there can be no respect for cultivated inwardness, no tolerance for an aristocratic method, because there is no established social activity for criticizing and assessing claims to cultivation according to standards of cultivation; there is no tradition of wisdom based on a system of education that instills it.

But wait a moment. The civil savage (who I am) does not want that sort of respect. It is better for him to live with these doubts and to be free of any particular tradition, to be able to relativize all traditions, to see through to the essence of all civilizations, and then to plunder the treasures of each one of them, at its source, as the liberated interpreter, the purest Protestant of all. If he can never be sure that he has actually discovered the treasures, but might, instead, only have given vent to himself, he can temper his doubts with a dash of common sense, realizing that even in a postcivilized society he still converses with other individuals, exchanging experiences and not just words with them. So why might he not receive experience from the texts of the world civilizations and then offer it to those among his contemporaries who are willing to accept it in the interest of their own fullness of life?

A more serious or at least more deeply felt objection to my approach to civilization is that even if I have achieved genuine and somewhat accurate insight, it is insight into an experience that very few human beings in any civilization have enjoyed and that is not reflective of how inwardness is lived generally in what have been called civilizations in a larger sense. How many Christians go through the agony of Paul of Tarsus, how many Hindus achieve unity with the One, and how many Athenians participated in the Platonic forms? Indeed, can one demonstrate any significant relation between the documents of the civilized elite and the lives of the broader population, except their use as ideologies legitimating domination and the translation of their symbols into external myth and ritual, providing support for magic, communal solidarity, and compensatory escapes from the trials of mundane existence? I have no answer to these questions. I surely do not hold that the everyday life of civilized societies is an emanation of a spiritual dialectic, yet I believe that the specific variants of that dialectic, expressed in world civilizations, provided an orientation or a focus for other cultural endeavors, such as the arts, the sciences, and the law, which are close to everyday life. I shall not support this conviction here but shall proceed as if it were true, evidencing it by my own experience of how the civilized mind in each instance intelligibly organizes life.

Let us begin our tour with all of the doubts and caveats in mind, because if there is one thing that differentiates the civil savage from his noncivil and uncivil brethren it is an acknowledgment of, indeed, an assent to, uncertainty about the most important matters, a self-assured irony betokening an embrace of the stubborn finitude that appears as the form of life. Our first stop is the civilization of East Asia, which comprehends a wide variety of spiritual impulses, including Confucianism, Taoism, and Buddhism. I find the essence of that civilization in Taoism, specifically in the *Tao-te-Ching*, which articulates a solution to the problem of being and goodness that is uniquely radical and unduplicated by any of the other world civilizations, a transcendence of convention and the self through the intimately aesthetic. Taoism is the path of trust in actuality or concretion, and, thus, is the abandonment of the separation of spirit from nature or, in more familiar and less accurate terms, of mind from body. It is the most thoroughgoing naturalism ever conceived by human thought, involving, paradoxically, a most strenuous discipline of relaxation, the fruits of which today are the demanding arts of Zen, each of which is perfected in liberated spontaneity, but achieves that release through painstaking training. ''Relax and ye shall find'' is the Taoist commandment, so difficult to obey, especially for the anxious modern spirit.

There is a large element of wit in even the profoundest inward agonies of East Asian civilization, which follows from the way in which the self is revealed to itself when it becomes separated from the daily round of communal existence. Have you ever become aware of yourself at a moment in which you were too full of yourself, overflowing with yourself? Perhaps you were self-righteously hectoring someone about some evil or grievance, or you were filled with the overriding importance of some task and would brook no opposition or obstacle, or you were just plunged into anxiety over some future event or into hope for some fulfillment. Then suddenly you saw yourself from the outside and were struck by your disproportion to the world, by the pathos of your earnestness, striving, and expectation, so futile when measured against the immense power of the world, which goes its own way whether or not you exist, whether or not you happen to like its way. This is the moment of separation and individualization for Taoism and, more generally, for East Asian civilization. Relive that experience, hold it close to you though it is painful, and you will feel humiliated in your own eyes, but it will not be an abject humility. Indeed, you may begin to smile ironically and marvel at how you could ever have been so pretentious.

Taoism is the tragicomedy of acknowledging pretense, that is, of recognizing pre-tension, centering the world around one's special desires, interests, and concerns, and staking one's being on one's sense of self-importance and self-will. East Asian cultures are often thought to be oriented through the sense of shame. In Taoism, that shame becomes self-referential: I become ashamed of myself, not just for some particular unseemly act or thought, but for the unseemliness of self-importance. Yet such a comprehensive emotional criticism carries with it no regret but an easy laughter. What could one have done? Foolishness is a pandemic. This is just what other civilized minds find it difficult to accept and what makes for the judgment that East Asian civilizations never birthed the full human individual. What a perverse and viciously naive judgment that is. The self is fully related to itself, completely detached from communal relation in its moment of self-humiliation, and if its sense of self-importance is dissolved then, the ego, as tautness of attention, becomes ever so much more powerful. Weak sense of self and strong ego is the formula of East Asian civilization and the secret of its contemporary success, the deep source of its cooperative technological order and of its lucid competitive spirit.

The recognition of the vanity of self-importance leaves the self suspended between its own desires, now revealed as presumptuous, and the self-generated creativity of the world, of nature, which is not merely external but which streams through the body as the dynamic feeling of life. The Taoist self breaks out of this suspended state by joining forces with nature and obliterating pretension. "Being is good" is interpreted as "nature is good": one submits to the creative dynamism of the world, becoming coincident and continuous with it, surrendering the distinction of one's will from it. This is the perfection of Taoism, the *wei-wu-wei*, which might best be translated as "do nothingness."[1]

To "do nothingness" does not mean to do nothing, but rather to refrain from attempting to organize the world to satisfy one's private hopes and to fend off one's fears; that is, not even to refrain from hoping and fearing, which are natural dispositions, but to make those emotions aspects only of the present moment and, thus, to neutralize them, to live them as actuality and not to identify the ego or spirit with them. So, in Zen, the fruition of doing nothingness, there is a generous, seemingly inhuman, acceptance of all natural appearance. According to the contemporary master Hasegawa, a fulfillment of the way would be to compose haiku in one's death agony: nature is good and the perfected life will rejoice in what it offers, not perhaps through praise, but through deeply appropriate, wholehearted response.

The radical identification with nature prescribed by Taoism leaves it with a difficulty in reconnecting with community where work must be done and self-importance cultivated through conventional systems of reward and punishment. In its original form, the politics of Taoism was anarchy, the return to the simple life of the village and, perhaps, the forest. Even Confucianism, which proclaimed the naturalness of convention, enunciated as its political ideal that the emperor should arrange public affairs so harmoniously that he could "let the robes fall," that is, abolish the symbols and substance of rule. All through East Asian civilization is the root belief that nature, whether immediately apprehended, as in Taoism, or cultivated, as in Confucianism and Zen, is a self-sufficient and trustworthy guide to life and that its negation is self-will, which cannot impair nature but must destroy itself. This belief is not implied in the moment of separation, in which the self is humbled before itself and acknowledges its radical insufficiency through the response of existential shame, but is based on the moment of submission, of the *wei-wu-wei*, letting nature take its course, "letting-be" and "setting-free," in Martin Heidegger's sense. The result of this submission turns out to be a heroism of experience, because it is ever so difficult for the self to affirm that the adversity it must suffer is good. The civil savage takes from East Asia the shame over all of the tricks of self-importance to cover up radical insufficiency and practices *wei-wu-wei* only when it is pleasant (all of the moments of erotic release) or opportune (all of the times when nature overwhelms the self) to do so.

Taoism is for the extremes of life, not the in-betweens, and the civil savage is, in Georg Simmel's term, a frontier being.

It is a daring strategy, prescribed by no other world civilization, to transcend the communal by throwing oneself back on the very nature that seems to have begged, by virtue of its incompletion and imperfection in our bodies, for supplementation by the contrivances of culture. Surely modernity has proceeded in the very opposite direction, staking everything at last, in the twentieth century, on technological compensation for biological failure. Indeed, the Taoist strategy only works if one lives moment by moment, identifying the self not with any continuous apprehension, but with its concrete response here and now, leaving the ego free to be pure awareness, no-mind. The purest of the East Asian philosophies is the heterodox variety of Zen called "momentalism" by D. T. Suzuki, which repudiates the orthodox category of eternal creative being and dissolves reality into a chain of lived present moments. Short of this austere reduction are all sorts of compromises with self-importance, the simplest and subtlest being the notion that each moment is a piece of eternity. From here life takes on a significance, the spirit informing an ethic of carefulness and adequate response to each situation, based on a vision of the solidarity of all beings in the eternal creative flow. The social principle of harmony and mutual adjustment follows upon this intuition and a culture prizing elegance, tact, the strength of restraint, and trained spontaneity grows around it. Today this culture must enter a pact with technology, which, in principle, brooks no limitation. The struggle is now in process, the severe test of East Asian cultures is underway.

East Asian civilization is the civilization of beauty, the one that cherishes a proportion and harmony transcending art and that the arts are intended to approximate. An aesthetic intimacy, an intuition of fitness and appropriateness, guides the civilized mind of the Far East in its search to overcome the alienation of the separate self, a transcendence of the everyday through immanence. When we move to the next stop on our tour, the Indian subcontinent, we notice a distinct change, which will set the pattern for all of the other civilizations we will discuss: the denial of the sufficiency of nature and the effort to root transcendence in an extramundane reality. For East Asian civilization, the secret of life is to become congruent with the reality of sense and feeling, whereas for the Hindu civilization that reality is deceptive, sometimes an illusion (nondualism, or *advaita*) and sometimes an inferior or deprived form of being (dualism, or *dvaita*). The keynote of Hindu civilization is the quest for the unity of the self with the source of its existence in an absolute being, which may be interpreted idealistically as an all-embracing self or may simply remain unnamed, because any designation would make it seem to be a particular, relative to other entities, and not ''that which is.''

In its striving for an extramundane transcendence, Hinduism is, perhaps, more uncompromising than is any other world civilization, but it is not unique in that search, sharing it with the religions of Jerusalem and with the Platonic strand of classical Greek thought. Its uniqueness lies in its comprehensiveness, in its total acceptance of every aspect of human existence in a spirit of thoroughgoing realism. Hinduism, indeed, is the only civilization that has provided a disciplined, philosophical reflection on the sexual impulse and its expression, most available in the West in the *Kama Sutra*, which is but one text in a rich literature on that theme. No other civilization has reflected on the human body so directly, has fused exercise with speculation, as the Hindu has through the discipline of Hatha yoga. Even the most spiritual of the works of Hindu civilization, the *Upanishads*, move through the concrete to the transcendent, counseling a variety of disciplines ranging from the mantra (the concreteness of speech) to entertaining metaphysical antinomies (the concreteness of reason). Throughout the range of its expressions, Hindu civilization is refreshingly free from piety: the dimensions of human life are revealed with an unillusioned attitude and they are admitted with the courage of tolerance, perhaps because they are not judged to be final. For example, the discipline of Hatha yoga seeks initially the unity of spirit and flesh through a living-into the flesh, its perfection through exercise aiming at a harmony of organic function, only to use that unity as a springboard to the supersession of flesh, a union of self with absolute being. Similarly, the passional union prescribed in the *Kama Sutra* is meant to be a symbol of ultimate union and an incitement to it. The most far-reaching metaphysical speculations are undertaken to show the insufficiency of reason and its collapse into antinomic contradiction, when it seeks to comprehend being itself. East Asia transcends into immanence, whereas India transcends out of immanence; these are two opposite strategies that, when perfected, may lead to the same kind of alert, attentive relaxation: in practicing Hatha yoga one must be ''firm and relaxed,'' and in performing the Chinese discipline of Tai Chi one must be ''steady and unbraced.'' Yet on the way to that goal there are great differences: Hinduism goes straight for self-control, not for "doing nothingness."

I shall take as my central text for understanding Hindu civilization the *Bhagavad-Gita*, which, like the *Tao-te-Ching*, is a work on political rule, best understood as reflecting on self-rule. In contrast to Taoism, where the self becomes separated from the everyday through a recognition of the absurdity of its self-importance in the face of nature, here the moment of severance is the far more frequent, indeed, ubiquitous experience of frustrated desire. The *Gita* is a conversation between the warrior Arjuna and the god Krsna (Krishna), who may be taken as figures representing, respectively, the active self immersed in the round of communal life and the observing ego. Arjuna is obliged to fight a battle in which many of his relatives are on the opposing side and he is agonized by the conflict between his duty and his love. Krsna attempts to persuade Arjuna to discharge his obligations as a warrior, but does not do so by a simple appeal to convention. Instead he raises Arjuna to an extreme individualization, showing him that no mundane desire is sufficient to satisfy the demands of human life, that immersing oneself in the *gunas*, or "strands," of life energy leads one on a downward spiral into a condition of opacity toward oneself, a self-contradicted solipsism, what we would call today schizophrenia. The individualization wrought by Krsna on Arjuna is radical because it does not merely criticize certain imprudent or evil desires, but relativizes all desire in terms of the insufficiency of its satisfactions: the self cannot remain satisfied with any finite fulfillment and, therefore, comes to itself only when it becomes detached from the objects of hope and fear; it is drawn inward and no longer is extended outside itself into the world.

However, it is not enough to remain in a state of suspension as a creature of desire who knows that his desires deceive him, as a radically insufficient or, as Alfred North Whitehead put it, ill-construed being. Krsna leads Arjuna toward union with the One, describing the various disciplines of Hindu civilization that both liberate the self from attachment to worldly concerns and reground it in its absolute source, in which being and goodness are fused. Yet just here the work takes a strange and special turn, deconstructing itself, revealing raw truth in a way that few other documents of elite civilization do so pointedly. Arjuna asks Krsna to vouchsafe to him the vision of absolute being, the "universal vision," which has never before been granted to a human self. Krsna complies and Arjuna is unable to tolerate it in its horror and magnificence. He begs Krsna to return to his benign and beneficent form, which the god does. Here is the lesson that human beings need to believe that being is good, though actually it is beyond good and evil, including both good and evil, and, perhaps, surpassing them in some unthinkable way. The entire corpus of Hindu disciplines is on trial here. What do these disciplines accomplish? Do they lead us merely to the reality that is good for us and not the absolute?

From the universal vision there is no way back to the community. Such reconnection is only possible through the peace provided by the vision of the good aspect of Krsna. On that basis Arjuna can be persuaded to fight because he can live within the equanimity, the indifference of the observing ego, and participate, through the active self, in the world by following the policy or strategy of "nonfruitive action"; that is, to do his duty according to the requirements of convention without worrying about the consequences. Here the moment of reconnection is presented with elegant simplicity: one takes up one's communal role just as one would have as a fully socialized being, but now in complete independence of any of the sanctions that motivate and provide incentives to those who are still immersed in the community.

In this perfect portrayal of the dynamics of premodern civilization, the enlightened individual returns to society as the strongest of its supports, enhanced by sharing in a greater reality. This is the romance of civilization, to be fully in the world, a valued contributor to the community, but not of it and, therefore, stronger and more reliable than those who are wholly committed to everydayness: a dream that is held ironically in the text that articulates it most perfectly. Awakened from this dream, the civil savage stakes himself on the universal vision, adopting the finite disciplines of militant and erotic unification, aware always that these disciplines never fully satisfy, but grateful for the difficult pleasures they nonetheless provide.

Muslim civilization, the next stop on our tour, is the most recent of the world civilizations, proclaiming itself the fruit of the last message of the God of Jerusalem, the same God who was revealed to the Jews and to Jesus. Here we encounter a dynamic of spirit that is far more familiar to the Western mind than are the dialectics of East Asian and Hindu civilizations, which seem not to place primary emphasis on the moral will, but individualize the self in relation to an impersonal reality or at least a marvelously subtle kind of being, which includes, fused within its integrity, personality and its antithesis, some kind of super-personality. The difference between the personal God of Jerusalem, who dialogues with believers, and the less-personalized absolutes of the East may be more of degree than of kind, at least in the case of Islam. Muslim civilization has achieved its greatest successes, historically, moving eastward, through Persia, Central Asia, and beyond, assimilating, rather than merely adding, elements of civilizations that originated in the stations along its path. Such assimilating and synthesizing was not merely a matter of the historical accidents of military and political power, but much more of a native and inherent affinity. The essence of Islam is *tawhid*, the perfect unity of Allah, which cannot be described adequately in human terms. The *kalma*, the credo of the muslim, states: "There is no God but God, and Muhammad is his messenger." That is, Allah is revealed in the manner that is appropriate for human beings. The way to direct knowledge of the absolute is closed: there is no fusion of finite self with the creative principle of being, as in Taoism, and no revelation of the universal vision, as there was for Arjuna in the *Gita*. Muhammad brings the message that Allah deems proper, a "plain warning and reminder" of the strict yet simple duties that human beings must discharge. Yet the *Koran* also announces that Allah "can do anything," that Allah has complete, unfettered command over creation, and that human beings are "vice-gerents" in the earth, cocreators with God and, therefore, commanders on their own accounts. The permission, indeed, obligation to command, and the supreme majesty of Allah, which makes even Allah's message perhaps provisional, opens the door wide to temptations to transcend to a reality beyond good and evil, providing thereby the restless and productive ferment in Islam and its internal connection to the civilizations of Asia.

The radical individualization of the self—its separation from communal bonds—is most starkly portrayed in the two world religions of Jerusalem, Christianity and Islam, because they seek to provide new models for the relation of self to other, not merely a new spirit to infuse the old relations. Nowhere is that portrayal of indigent separation more elegantly stated than in the *Koran*, where the natural man, stripped of his myths and illusions, must confront himself in the utter privacy of his spiritual existence: "Lo! Man was created anxious; fretful when evil befalleth him and when good befalleth him grudging." Islam, at its profound core, is the most existential of the world civilizations, uncompromising in its insistence that the individual acknowledge that self-disclosed life is made of anxiety and fear, and that the self is constituted by a deficit of power. Here is what lies beneath the vanity of self-importance revealed by Taoism and the futility of desire announced by Hinduism: the sheer inability, due to the individual's constitutive weakness, to tolerate adversity and to enjoy success. It is Islam's unique contribution to have discovered that the root of the self's predicament is the problem of self-rule, that is, of command over the forces within the self that take it away from itself. Islam makes the perplexity of anxiety extreme by asserting that the individual's salvation is completely a matter between God and the self: no one can take charge of another's eternal destiny nor is any intercession possible. Thus, within the sphere of self-enclosed privacy shot through with anxiety, the self must somehow take charge.

The existential structure of Islam is evinced in its interpretation of the act of faith, which regrounds the self as a steadfast follower of Allah, worshipful and obedient to Allah's message. Islam means submission, which is deemed to be the only way in which the individual can overcome natural anxiety. This submission has been grievously misunderstood in the West to bespeak a surrender of will resulting in either a fanatical self-transcendence or a quietistic fatality. Surely some muslims have lived their faith in this way, just as members of each of the other civilized cultures have appropriated the spiritual dialectic to mask and to cater to the frailty of the self. For the *Koran,* submission is quite the opposite of abandonment: it is self-surrender, undertaken and consummated with the most lucid self-consciousness, a free act of will, not a conversion, but rather a response to a plain warning and reminder, not a supersession of self.

The thoroughgoing respect for the individual ego in Islam has led, as it assimilated aspects of Persian and Hindu civilizations, to a unique form of mysticism that glorifies self-command and breaks even the bond of submission, deconstructing the faith in a manner similar to the deconstruction of Zen by momentalism and of Hinduism by the universal vision.

The early Persian mystics, the progenitors of Sufism, made the bold experiment of surrendering the self to the self. The most pregnant expression of this pure self-relation was enunciated by Hallaj: ''I am the creative truth.'' Let these words penetrate your experience and you may find that you are seized with an overwhelming sense of your indubitable concrete reality. Indeed, grasp yourself as living, here and now, under the revelatory power of Hallaj's words, of his declaration-deed, and you may intuit that the status of being itself is nothing but your current doing: reality is a process of creation and you are a cocreator, along with every other center of initiative. Muhammad declared that he was time itself. Each of us gives time its substance, each one of us is the truth of being, and we can become coincident with that truth at any instant. This is the most sublime and holy arrogance: the cramp in my finger, the chill from the ill-heated room, and the thoughts of these are the truth of being. One need not listen for Being, as Heidegger did, for it is here in each movement, in each doing. It is just this truth that the *Koran* says we cannot tolerate and yet it is the truth that the civilization of the *Koran* precipitated: in coming to myself I come to being. There is no greater liberation than to be surrendered to one's own reality, having abolished distance from oneself, and there is no greater torture, because even one's anxiety is creative truth. It is no wonder that the authorities executed Hallaj; his declaration-deed is the credo of the civil savage.

Orthodox Islam, of course, does not prescribe self-surrender to the commanding ego, but to Allah and Allah's message. There is no way back to community from the seizure of the self as creative truth; the only way open is toward the community of muslims informed by submission to the message, which is a program of obligations for constituting that community, backed by the promise of paradise and the warning of hell. These duties, prescribing mercy, justice, and benevolence, are meant to be within the scope of normal human capacity and are offered not in an austere and demanding spirit, but charitably: one should orient one's life toward their discharge, but should not be too harsh on oneself if one succumbs to weakness now and then. The Koranic spirit is one of justice tempered with mercy or, in its greatest moments, of mercy tempered with justice. The fruition of orthodox Islam, whether Sunni or Shi'a, in a good yet humanly possible community, is what gives it appeal in the contemporary world. Islam is a living civilization in a world that is becoming postcivilized, the going alternative to postcivilized modernity.

⇨

To this point we have been moving westward through the great civilizations in a geographical order, but now we will make a detour to ancient Athens before exploring the Christianity of Paul of Tarsus and then our own modern civilization. One of the great themes of twentieth-century thought prior to World War II was that of the constitution of modernity through the contributions of Athens and Jerusalem. Indeed, a sign of the unmaking of the modern—its deconstruction—was the appearance in our century of the thematization of civilization, beginning after World War I with Oswald Spengler's *Decline of the West* and then taken up far more profoundly by such Russian thinkers as Lev Chestov and Pitirim Sorokin, the British philosopher-historians Arnold Toynbee and R. G. Collingwood, the Spaniards Miguel de Unamuno and José Ortega, and the Americans F.S.C. Northrop and Stephen Pepper. These and many other similar efforts were undertaken in the spirit of discovering what had made the modern West unique and to defend that uniqueness against Walter Rathenau's "vertical barbarians," the new, noncivilized masses, and from the impact of other world civilizations, which were being drawn into the orbit of the West economically, technologically, and militarily. This moment of philosophy of civilization, filled with attempts at finding a preeminence for the West or for composing syntheses of the world civilizations, now appears to be a grand retrospective on the era in human history of civilization itself. Yet it leaves the lasting contribution of having defined modernity through, as Unamuno put it best in *The Agony of Christianity*, an uneasy combination of Greek rationalism and Christian freedom, a dialectic of the static and dynamic. I address Greek civilization first because I believe that it is the counterpoint to the Christian theme of modernity, the limitation to the wild element in Christianity, which, after Paul's criticism of the Judaic law, takes the place of that law as a moderator of freedom.

Athenian and, more generally, pre-Christian, Greco-Roman civilization bear great resemblance to the civilizations of East Asia and the Indian subcontinent, particularly in its Platonic expression, which was influenced by strains of Eastern mysticism. Indeed, the elemental structure of Athenian civilization, which appears in Plato's *Republic*, another work of political and self rule, follows the pattern of Hindu thought quite closely. *The Republic*, similarly to the *Gita*, may be interpreted as a reflection on the frustration of every desire but that for the ground of being. The Socrates of the Dialogues—however much his image changes as Plato becomes more confident of the singularity and integrity of his own ideas—remains a strange and compelling mixture of both wholehearted love for carnal desire and its satisfaction, and dedication to transcend such desire in the cause of grasping the truth of being, which is inseparable from the goodness of being. Socrates is one of the great individuals to have graced the earth, embodying in his life of combat, carnal love, discourse, and restless and courageous thought the paradigm of a civilized person. He radically individualized himself from communal convention by reflecting about it philosophically and by questioning the opinions of his fellows about good and evil, driving them to acknowledge that they nursed within them a better self that was directed toward a greater satisfaction than they were willing to recognize. He performed his task of midwife of the soul simply by showing others that they did not really want what they claimed to desire—power, wealth, and sensory gratification—because these goods were deceptive and their pursuit led the self to an insatiable, solipsistic, and alienated tyranny over itself, the same schizophrenia that the *Gita* recounts as the result of submission to the *gunas*. Fleshly desire, uncontrolled by an organizing principle, simultaneously drew the self hermetically inside itself through its futility, and outside itself through its anxious search for gratification. Authentic individualization arose from the simple act of questioning desire, which creates an emergent realm of thought, self-subsistent yet open to reality.

Radical individualization, for the Platonic Socrates, was accomplished through thinking, not through the emotion of shame, the intuition of passion's limits and frustrations, or the apprehension of the anxious will. The Greek legacy to the individual is doubt and irony, and in the early Dialogues, perhaps best in *The Protagoras*, Socrates seems to live in that humbling doubt about the powers of thought to determine truth, which bears with it the confidence that one can at least grasp the inadequacy of one's opinions, a kind of epistemic existentialism that attracted Søren Kierkegaard among the moderns. This is the Socratic equivalent of the *Koran*'s natural man, who exists in anxiety. However, Plato did not allow his Socrates to halt at this moment of the intellectualized spirit, which is where the civil savage embraces Socrates, identifying him with the famous irony that the wisest are those who know that they do not know, yet with the necessary addition that bound up with conscious life are stubborn assents about what it means. Plato's dissatisfaction with arrogant doubting is evinced in his new ground for the spirit, beyond the community in the forms of things, apprehended by the intellect. The realm of forms—which guarantees that reality is the way it should be and that being is good—is the origin of Western rationalism, the dream and romance that thinking is the royal road to the good life and that the discoveries of the intellect are the models for social practice. Here is the difference between *The Republic* and the *Gita*. Arjuna returns to fight his battle and to discharge his conventional obligations strengthened by the independence of the "knower" (ego) from the "field" (body and its passions); alternatively, Plato's Guardian returns to the community with a proper pattern for its organization based on apprehension of the forms and their unification in the idea of the good. For Hindu civilization the intellect itself is an aspect of the field, a tool of the passions that must be pushed into the field on the path toward the One. That Plato and his Socrates severed the intellect from the field and identified it with the knower was fateful for the West, setting it with hope on a course that thinking can resolve the frailties of existence. Today we see this has issued in the madness of the technological remaking of nature.

Plato was not a dynamic, technological rationalist. Although in principle the good life was possible to institute under a reign of justice—balancing temperance, courage, and wisdom in the soul, and craft, administration, and governance in the state—Plato's experiment in Syracuse was a failure and one suspects that he never altogether escaped the influence of Socratic irony. There is a wistfulness to his hypothetical statement "if philosophers were kings or kings philosophers." There is an inherent rupture between the philosopher's kingdom of the intellect and the perceptual world of the public square, in which diversity of opinion bursts forth from the inadequacies of existence, inexpungable. Indeed, the return of the regrounded self to the community is best expressed in the Dialogues where the death of Socrates is discussed, the *Apology*, *Crito*, and *Phaedo*. Here Socrates, convicted by his fellow citizens of corrupting the youth by leading them to question communal convention, refuses the pleas of his friends to accept exile and insists upon drinking the hemlock because of his piety toward Athens, which through its *nomos* and *ethos* gave him his very being, his possibility to become an individual. Socratic piety is the counterpart of Socratic irony, the first tempering the second so that it never escapes fully from the social bond, as a fuller-strength freedom might. The death of Socrates ties Plato more closely to the *Gita* than do the speculations of *The Republic*, because Socrates takes his punishment with his soul directed toward the form of the good, finally indifferent to the consequences of temporal affairs on him and willing to accept the judgments of those who work the community's conventions. Perhaps the civil savage should accept Socrates at his word, even the Platonic Socrates: how much irony might there be in this piety?

Now let us turn back to Jerusalem for the last stop on our tour of the premodern civilizations, Christianity. This is the most difficult part of my free meditation, one that I cannot approach with the same detachment that I have been able to maintain toward the other great world civilizations, even toward the modern, which contains such a strong dose of rationalism that I am often prompted to smile at it forgivingly for its intellectual illusion, so comforting if also so brutally perverse when it stakes its pretensions on science. Christianity, however, is anything but comforting to me, and in these reflections I must be personal, since Christianity is the most intimately personal of all religions. It is profoundly disquieting, the wild card of the human spirit that disturbs all calculations by setting spirit in direct relation to flesh and making both seethe with the desire to overcome, yet holding fast to the pleasure palace and torture chamber that is bodily existence.

The more I study the national traditions of modern philosophy, the more convinced I become that they are secularized adaptations of some form of Christianity. As George Santayana noted, for example, American idealism and pragmatism are philosophical translations of Puritanism. If modern civilization is extinct, it is because it has been de-Christianized: the fine balance that modern civilization must maintain between reason and freedom has been deranged by the enfeebling and denaturing of its dynamic component, the freedom expressed in the carnal hunger for salvation from the flesh for the flesh. As a twentieth-century intellectual I am awash in the detritus of Christian civilization, which is tossed about everywhere by the currents of modern doctrine. As I seek the core of Christianity, I am not drawn towards Jesus but to that all-too-human individual, Paul of Tarsus, who so often seems to need the ministrations of that other dissatisfied Jew, Sigmund Freud. I could meditate with great joy on the Jesus of the Gospels, sometimes Taoist when he counsels to be as ''the lilies of the field,'' sometimes Hindu when he prescribes a life in the world but not of it, enunciator of the dialectic of civilization when he reminds us that we gain the self by losing it, and finally the deconstructionist word become flesh when he asks God why he has been forsaken as he dies on the cross. For me, Jesus is the last of God's abused prophets, a latter-day Jonah who uneasily pays the price for following his Lord's command. Yet from Jesus we do not proceed to modernity. It is Paul, the apostle to the gentiles, who leads us to ourselves. He is the secret of Western individualism, covered over by our forgetfulness.

Paul is the agonist of community, the one who proclaims the tragedy of society. Radical individualization and separation from communal bonds is in his case so extreme that it finally results in the hysterical neurosis of temporary blindness. He does not mock his self-importance in the Taoist manner, reflect upon the worth of his desires as Socrates did, or encounter futility or anxiety, but wrestles directly with his insufficiency in relation to the demands of his community, the Jews, who have been bestowed with the gift-curse of being chosen to adhere to God's law. Paul is the persecutor of the Christians because he is not able to lead a sinless life, the perfect exemplar of the fanatic who projects his weakness on the other so that he can avoid confronting himself. This is not a piece of speculative psychoanalysis, but is Paul's own judgment of his practice when he reviews it after his conversion, after he has recovered from the breakdown on the road to Damascus and has received the spirit. The cruel reflections on the law that appear in the Epistle to the Romans are the birth pangs of modern existentialism, which set a pattern that will be carried forward from Augustine through Blaise Pascal to Kierkegaard and then on to Friedrich Nietzsche, who is the Paul of modernity, the suffering spirit incarcerated in the suffering flesh who witnesses the "last man" blinking with self-satisfaction and trampling upon the seriousness of life.

I know of nothing more cruel and brutal in world literature than Paul on the law. In his view the natural man, who has not lived with the gift-curse of God's law, does not sin. He may, indeed, incur punishment for his deeds from the protectors of the communal order and will surely suffer the physical and emotional consequences of his choices, but he will not experience the added agony of apprehending his own depravity. Here is the extreme individualization of guilt, of what Feodor Dostoevsky called self-laceration, fully private, the gnawing and nagging loneliness that still drives the modern herd-people to escape from themselves into the clutches of others, who, in turn, are consumed by the same self-hatred.

Why not just consider this a local neurosis of Jewish culture, as Nietzsche was so often tempted to conclude? Such a simplification will not, unfortunately, do. Perhaps, I should say fortunately, because the civil savage prizes this guilt, which is the gateway to the free body, the wild flesh, restrained only by a dreadfully fragile conscience and fruitfully unbalanced by the impossible will to be more than itself; as another uneasy Jew, Georg Simmel, put it, life is "more life" and "more-than-life."

The only way to deny Paul's agony, for a modern, is to become the "last man." I need not accept God's law to be assured of my sin; any standard that I have taken deeply into myself, that has formed my bridge to living-into the world, will do once the Pauline legacy has been transmitted to me, as it has been to the modern Western individual. Surely, I can make the bold experiment, undertaken explicitly by Nietzsche and more tacitly by Freud, of anaesthetizing or of surgically removing the superego, but that will only leave me with the very flesh that has been revealed as inadequate to conscience: it will not magically remove that inadequacy, since the real gift-curse is, first, that the flesh is insufficient to the culture it creates, and, second, that culture stubbornly obtrudes itself as Simmel's more-than-life. My only alternative, again, is to become the last man, to feed off the reassurances of the mass media, to externalize myself into the technological imagination of the electrified chatter, television and radio. I choose Paul's agony, with the liberating insight that the spirit may learn to tolerate the wayward flesh, to glory in depravity even as spirit turns toward flesh with a steady will to discipline what can never be sanely disciplined but only repressed. The civil savage will not repress.

Did Paul repress? I will not spend much time on his regrounding of the self and his reconnection with community because here I can speak with no inward authority. The West knows that Paul recovered from his hysteria by receiving the spirit and becoming a new man in Christ. I have not received grace nor am I living in disposition toward it, so I can claim only imperfect understanding of those civilizations that depend on the spiritual initiatives of the individual and no intimate understanding of the one that relies upon conversion. The regrounding in a gift of the spirit, which allows one both to throw off the old Adam and bring faith, hope, and love into the community (as Paul tried to do for the Western churches), is intelligible to me only through its external expressions. I know only that the life of postcivilized America, which I share, is not Christian in the Pauline sense, but that it is shot through with grotesquely pitiful efforts to elude the Pauline predicament of the guilt that springs from inadequacy. We cannot save ourselves, and without the gift of spirit we are cripples leaning on each other. This is the result of the modern project of killing God. Nietzsche understood this more than dimly, but he pitted the overman against the last man in a final romantic gesture. The civil savage prefers the project of tolerating the agonized Paul, just as he favors Jesus on the cross at his moment of radical doubt: a resurrectionless and unredeemed Christianity, suspended in total freedom, and human self-revelation between the law and the prophets, and the Christ.

⌂

Now we are ready to complete our tour, which has really been a mission of appreciative plunder, in what the Mexican philosopher

Leopoldo Zea calls "the Occident," which was formed by the leading nations of England, France, and Germany. I shall pass over that transitional civilization, the medieval, which had no distinctive structure of spirit of its own, but which was a series of efforts to integrate the contributions of Athens and Jerusalem into a unitary life formed by the Christian theme. Modern civilization, in the wake of which we live, has been distinguished from all of the other great world civilizations by what Karl Mannheim called "the dynamic insight," the intuition of being as a process of continuous qualitative change. However, even deeper than this insight and grounding it, I believe, is a spirit of profound restlessness, which has been ever dissatisfied with consolations, compensations, and the very touchstone of civilization, a formula for equating being and goodness.

The searching spirit of the West has been evinced, even more than by a privileging of the sense of time, by an openness to difference, by a bursting of the bonds of form, whether attachment to form be expressed through embrace of present novelty, future possibility, past achievements, or accomplishments of other civilizations. Modernity is essentially a process of growth into the world as a totality of differences, a maturation of the human spirit to the point at which it unembarrasses itself of any fixed forms of order at all and is finally plunged into the fateful crisis of either moving on to tolerate the diversity of life (the universal vision incarnate), or to fabricate through its own collective imagination, the mass media of communication, a self-conscious dream (the beneficent and benevolent Krsna become celebrity). Modernity is the gradual emergence of the fleshly agony of Paul of Tarsus from the cocoon of Platonic ideas in which it had been wrapped, the precipitation of concrete individuality from its fluid social medium. The most concrete individuality is also the most comprehensive and promiscuous individuality, and also the most crystalline. I am following and extending here the intimations of Georg Simmel in his essay "The Conflict of Modern Culture," which proposes that the modern theme is the revelation of life to itself as a qualitative dynamic, ever resistant to capture by intellectual form, always lunging beyond itself only to fall back upon itself. In accord with such a perspective, then, there is no postmodern era, but instead only the vain and hideous effort to deny the demands of modernity that one be lucid about life and institute a form for life by invention and contrivance.

At the dawn of the modern period, the dynamic insight and the explosion of diversity in the fleshly spirit were not apparent in the ideas through which the spirit articulated its self-understanding, but they were inherent in the experience of individuals who formulated those ideas. Indeed, modernity may be understood as a process that took place of decivilizing the spirit as thought became progressively more intimately acquainted with life, and of attempting to heal the alienation of theory and practice, if only then to experience the acute and profound alienation of flesh from culture.

My text for early-modern civilization must be the introductory remarks in René Descartes's *Discourse on Method*, which form the ground plan for the two other great moments of modern Western civilization, those of Immanuel Kant and Nietzsche. Descartes is the exemplar of the restless modern spirit. He reports that he was impelled from his youth onward by a quest for certain knowledge because he wanted "to walk with confidence in this life." In such a quest is the profound scission between the Socratic individualization and the modern: Socrates sought the truth of goodness, whereas Descartes quested for knowledge that he could be sure would not deceive him, whatever it turned out to be. Descartes, like Socrates, questioned all of the prevailing opinions, first those of his Scholastic teachers, then those of the various European cultures to which he exposed himself, as he prosecuted his search through travel. Dissatisfied with all of the knowledge that he had gained except for the methods and findings of the natural sciences, he ended up in Holland at a loss about how to proceed. Withdrawing into a stove-heated room (prompting Unamuno to call him the "stove philosopher"), he decided to make himself his "own object of study." The results of his inquest, pregnant for modern civilization, are well known: Descartes discovered that he could be sure that he existed as a thinking being, because, though he might be deceived by his judgment of the status of any object of his thought, he could not be deceived that he was thinking that thought. The *cogito ergo sum* is the declaration of independence of the modern individual, the decommunalizing declaration-deed that frees the individual from any conventional attachments. From this intuition or intellection of a purely unqualified thinking substance, a cogitating ego, the individual must find a way back into the world and the flesh.

Descartes did not find a bridge to the other-than-self from his isolated thinking ego, which provided him with no resources to walk with confidence and none of the guides for conduct for which he had hoped. Instead, he became intoxicated with his discovery and created a firm dualism between theory and practice. Toward the world of finite and mutating social relations he adopted a "provisional morality," prescribing obedience to the regnant norms, just those opinions he had so

severely questioned throughout his previous years of search. Toward
perceptual reality he took the scientific approach, articulating the modern dream of a future biological science that would improve the quality
of human life, anticipating contemporary postcivilization, fascinated by
the "bionic man." Finally, he regrounded his lonely ego in a concept,
and created the myth of modern rationalism. Unlike the Platonic Socrates who was attracted to the idea of goodness erotically and almost
mystically, Descartes took a logical approach to transcendence, claiming that the fact that he could think the idea of a perfection, while he
acknowledged his own imperfection, showed that his abstract conception referred to a real existence. Here he returned to the ontological
argument of his Scholastic teachers that the lesser cannot of its own
power think the greater. So, the Cartesian solution, which is the paradigm of modern civilization, fell backward for its very ground and for
its connection to the other human being, and raced forward in its relation to the perceptual world of "extended substance." As it proceeded,
the modern spirit would abandon the metaphysical rationalism and the
provisional morality and would intensify its commitment to mathemati-
cal and experimental science. Most importantly, it would undertake a
long task of enriching the Cartesian thinking substance, injecting it with
morality and finally fleshing it out carnally, so that now a completely
concrete individual confronts the human works of technology with a
terrible fascination.

The next moment in the development of modern civilization is that
of Kant's transcendental philosophy. Indeed, Kant may be considered
the high point of modernity, standing between the early-modern en-
chantment with the rational idea and the late-modern absorption in the
flow of life. As a critic, Kant devised a "transcendental method,"
through which he showed that rational ideas, such as the Cartesian idea
of perfection, could not be proven to refer to any being independent of
the ego who thinks them. The concepts of the sciences did refer to
objects, but only as they appeared to perception: being-itself, the Cartesian ground for the ego, was inaccessible to human thought and was
one of the ideas of human reason that the ego had to think, but for
which the ego could not know the referent, if, indeed, there was one.
Thus did Kant deprive modern civilization of its connection to all of
the premodern civilizations, a transcendental ground reconnecting the

self that had been separated from its communal ties to a greater reality. Kant's more important contribution lies in the far more productive direction of moralizing the Cartesian ego. Finding the path to the absolute blocked to theoretical cognition, Kant turned to social life, which Descartes had left in a provisional status, and introduced the conception of a practical reason that provides guidance to conduct solely on the basis of an inward apprehension. His radicalization of the individual is through the introjection of the will, which is left by itself to determine its principle of conduct, how it is to dispose itself to itself and to others.

For Kant, it is possible to walk with confidence in this life, because reason supplies to the will a "categorical imperative" to choose only those actions that can be universalized to all wills, the rationalist translation of the Christian law of love to do unto others as you would have them do unto you. Kant acknowledges, however, that his imperative falls within the province of a "rational being," who is swayed only by universal law, and is an aspiration for a concrete human being in the clutches of felt "inclinations" toward the objects of sense. Human beings as we encounter them are "unsociable social beings," which makes the life of the moral self a struggle, constituted by what Hegel called the "unhappy consciousness" of self-alienation, of never being at one with one's better self. The Cartesian ego becomes, in Kant's hands, the "end-in-itself," the very reason for being and doing, secured as such by its own intent to be moral, and inspired by a seamless system of ethical community, a "kingdom of ends." Yet this community is ideal and must remain so, and each of us must confront our inadequacy to that which is "written on our hearts." Paul of Tarsus returns with a vengeance, without the possibility of saving grace, a gift of spirit. The French Revolution posed socially the challenge of a moralized society and then Kant took that demand within the self. However, the self thus enriched had to learn that the fleshly spirit is weak. Kant understood this, but the nineteenth-century mind tried to reject it, and, for the most part, set out to moralize the community, ushering in the era of ideology. Yet dogging the steps of revolution and reform was the rebellion of the flesh, the growing insight that the end-in-itself is not the morally rational being constituted by the categorical imperative, but the unsociable social being, whom Unamuno called "the man of flesh and bone who is born, suffers, and dies."

What was to become of the will tortured by unhappy consciousness? The answer is provided by Nietzsche who stands at the final moment of modern civilization, its uneasy deconstructionist. Kant had begun the deconstruction of modern civilization by depriving rational ideas of a reference in objective reality. Throughout the early-modern period, Continental rationalism had been shadowed by its bad conscience, British empiricism, but, except for Bishop George Berkeley, the criticism of the line of thinkers from Thomas Hobbes through John Locke to David Hume had not attempted to clarify the limits of reason in all of the spheres of life, rigidifying, instead, the split between theory and practice consummated by the Cartesian revolution, and attending to the derivation of concept from percept. Only Kant dared to apply empirical criticism everywhere to discover just what could be affirmed by a self-lucid reason. His bold effort resulted in throwing the individual back upon the will. Descartes could equate being and goodness through the idea of perfection, given to the ego by a power greater than itself, but Kant, despite his positing a God to balance, as Max Weber put it, the moral bankbook, could finally proclaim only that the self should strive to be good, without any ground for confidence that reality was on its side.

Why should self be pledged to the categorical imperative? Here Nietzsche enters, declaring that the rationalized will is but a sublimation of the vital will to power, indeed, a neurotic distortion of it springing from resentment of the weak against strength, reflected mendaciously as the nobility of self-effacement. Thus, Nietzsche comes full circle to Paul of Tarsus struggling with the law before his conversion experience. The famous "death-of-God decree" announces the modern unmaking of its received grounds in the holy spirit and Platonic reason: we have been severed from the past by our own skeptical criticism and must henceforth live within our fleshly and mundane limitations, conscious that we give ourselves our laws out of our ever-fluctuating and uncertain vitality. Nietzsche glimpsed, often grasped, this conclusion, which puts an end to civilization, but he also sought in evolution a new criterion, an image of the overman, who would exalt joy in vitality and thereby overcome the agony of culture, the tensely anguished relation between the inspirited flesh and its ideals, which disclose to itself its own insufficiency.

Let us pass by Nietzsche's effort to ground modern civilization in the *nisus* toward a future perfection. We will encounter it again in its adulterated forms, the aspiration to a "new socialist man" or to perfection through biotechnology, both of which are unholy marriages of science and the self, thoroughly deindividualized prescriptions for an uncivil, technological savagery. Let us, instead, dwell for a moment on the radically individualized will to power, which has become fully conscious of the stubbornly factual limitations to its power and finds no consolation in some contribution it might make as a "bridge to the overman." The death of God, for Dostoevsky, meant that everything was possible because there were no longer any prohibitions on conduct. This is the conclusion of the newly uncivilized self who stares into the abyss of desire, wrenched by moral nihilism. Yet we can stand more firmly now, if we know that the Pauline predicament does not end with God's banishment. The motto of the civil savage is: Everything is possible, nothing is necessary. As long as we connect with the other-than-self we will do so through standards and forms. There is no connection that we have to make, no experience that we have to have; it is not even self-evident that we should try to satisfy our most insistent desires for they could deceive us. It might be better just to imagine their fulfillment. I am the creative truth, but there is no truth that it is necessary to create. There is nothing that I have to do, nothing that is necessarily good for me. I am even beyond the agony of having to decide, which plagued Jean-Paul Sartre: my body and psyche will decide for me, as long as I am alive and aware. I can let myself be lived by habit and the transient promptings of impulse. Hold yourself in this state of radical suspension and extreme individualization, beyond civilization because it has locked the doors to transcendence. After you have tasted this "zero point," which is where the civil savage dwells, accompany me on a new journey, into the technological jungle where we might learn to live, fight, and love, which is all that there is left to do for the postcivilized modern.

Chapter 2

Defensive Life

We are living in a remarkably privileged age for anyone who is able and willing to grasp its prime possibility, which is to live in full awareness of life as it is, unvarnished by any appeal to a transcendent reality. I do not deny that a minority of individuals who dwelt in the great world civilizations had access to life itself; indeed, within the spiritual dialectic of each civilization there is that moment in which the self is suspended in a condition of radical separation between the communal environment from which it arose and the new ground that it seeks in a greater reality. Yet that suspension is always provisional for the civilized mind, which even in its most profound uncertainties and agonies, nurses a hope for a transforming experience, which will place it on an even more secure and firm footing in the world. The novelty of the postcivilized modern mind is that its self-lucidity requires that it exist only toward everyday worldliness, but with acute acknowledgment of its stubborn limitations: the civil savage has assimilated the decommunalizing moment of civilization, in every one of its dimensions, but must return to everydayness without any compensation for the loss of community. The savage is the mature embodiment of the masterless man who so frightened the defenders of early-modern civilization, the offspring of Dostoevsky's "underground man," who encounters moral nihilism, and of Max Stirner's "ego," the insurrectionist against any sublimation of Stirner's "man of hide and hair."

Georg Simmel notes that the self-revelation of life was first achieved in the modern period in the "philosophy of life," which was founded by Arthur Schopenhauer. Working within the Kantian problematic of practical reason, Schopenhauer desublimated the morally rationalized will and encountered its foundation in the will to live, the ceaseless and restless process of seeking an object that would give it lasting satisfaction. He was the first thinker to burst the bonds of rationalism and Western thought, connecting with Hindu civilization through his doctrine of the insatiability of desire. Schopenhauer's will was boundless, but his imagination could only provide him with finite objects, all of which the will would quickly outrun. Suspension in frustration impelled Schopenhauer to attempt to deny the will, primarily through aesthetic contemplation. He was spared the Pauline agony because he had not penetrated radically enough to the core of life, which is the entrapment of the will in the body: in criticizing the Kantian will he had also dispensed with the ego; it was the metaphysical will of the world that was a useless passion, not himself, the flesh-and-bone man, Schopenhauer. So, in a move of Sartrian bad faith he could conceal himself from himself while contemplating the failure of the will. This depersonalization of spirit left Schopenhauer in a state of "boredom," which is the normal route of escape from the agony of the enfleshed spirit.

Those who followed in Schopenhauer's path of making life the object of thought could not so easily take his metaphysical flight and had to face the corporeality of will, the fusion of life and spirit in the mutating and desiring flesh. The pioneer who staked out the spirit's claim to the territory of the body was Nietzsche, who ventured beyond the mere fact of desire to the problem that it posed for the self of its control and direction. For the conscious self, if not for every organic expression of life, the will to live is the will to power, the impulse to integrate and command vital drive so that its release produces plenitude and joy. From the standpoint of the will to power, life is revealed, using Martin Heidegger's expression, "proximally and for the most part" as a dynamic of ascension and decline. Ascending life and declining life are the great divisions of unillusioned human existence, available, though never simultaneously, to introspection. As life ascends, its forces gather spontaneously into a dynamic unity and the self becomes capable of appreciating and enjoying all of what the experience of the world offers to it that it can assimilate; whereas in declining life the vital forces weaken and disperse, and the world becomes unfriendly, because the self must be involved in trying to gather its energies together, to repair the damage it senses as the impulse and temptation to reject being.

That the dynamic of life is constituted by an inherent dialectic of positivity and negativity, which grounds judgments of value prereflectively, was affirmed by many of Nietzsche's successors. Perhaps the most famous of them was Freud, whose metapsychology divided the life impulses first into Eros (unification) and Ananke (necessity), and later into Eros and Thanatos (dissolution). The difference between his two pairings is crucial to one's orientation toward life. The distinction between Eros and Thanatos is the poetic expression of metabolism and catabolism, which are thoroughly organic in their import; whereas that between Eros and Ananke is far more spiritual, differentiating the metabolic direction from the effort to preserve the organism from the threats to its integrity from within and without.

Eros and Thanatos are the signs of old age, and Eros and Ananke are the signs of middle age. Indeed, Freud's embrace of a ''death instinct'' betokens a surrender of the will to power, a lapse into Schopenhauer's passivity toward life, which, of course, is understandable for one who is caught in the spiral of declining life. The civil savage does not take death inside himself in a fatalistic way, because life is, for him, still an enterprise, though he admits that it is finally a losing proposition. He thinks and acts under the signs of Eros and Ananke, loving the finite perfections of experience and acknowledging severely the necessity that makes those perfections so limited. He is ready, however, when Ananke overwhelms, to admit the *wei-wu-wei*, the ''do nothingness'' of Thanatos.

When life is still, as Ortega calls it, a *quehacer*, a ''what to do'' or ''what is to be done,'' Thanatos does not appear as a tranquil admission of defeat through dispersion, but as a rebellion against the limitations of life, a terrible inability to tolerate all of the forces that unmake vitality, a horror at the three Buddhist evils of death, disease, and decay that is expressed as a hatred of existence itself. Perhaps the deepest intuition of the civil savage is that life is filled with adversity. His firmest judgments are that adversity itself is evil, that evil is in the world and not merely in the self, and that evil cannot be justified, certainly not rationally. However, he does not take the next and fateful step, which was the downfall of the underground man, Raskolnikov, Ivan Karamazov, and Herman Melville's Ahab, that of absorbing that evil into his spirit and of making war upon the world, himself, and other selves. It is not that being is good, for it is hardly that, but that depravity is so bad, not imprudent, because nothing is necessary, but just so unfortunate. Adversity become self-loathing turns back to create a loathsome world. Here we have nihilism in vivo, the one attitude toward existence that the civil savage will not take, and his renunciation is the essence of his civility. From that renunciation come both the affirmation of struggle and the struggle to affirm, which make up the civil savage's life.

⇩

However much we may attempt to remediate and obscure the radical adversity of personal existence, it remains as the foundation upon which any sane thinking about life must be built. Much of modern philosophy has been preoccupied, as a result of what Ralph Barton Perry called the "egocentric predicament" of the Cartesian method, with the problem of the existence of the external world. It is true that if I hold everything that appears to me relative to my consciousness of it, I cannot prove that there is anything outside the processes of my thinking. Yet even if I admit that I have access only to my version of the world, I assent even more confidently that it is not my world, that things are not the way I would like them to be. This real assent, which John Henry Newman called an unshakable belief, to constitutive imperfection is my best guarantee that reality outruns my consciousness of it. Each stress, strain, and pain that I feel shows me that I am an ill-construed organism, divided within itself, which is maladapted to its circumstances. The need to struggle to stay even with life is the gateway to reality, even if the humility of intellectual probity requires that I do not make quick and easy judgments about what that reality is made of and how exactly it is structured. All of the world civilizations acknowledge the limitations, fissures, and tensions of conscious life, as they try to sublimate, heal, and resolve them through discovering a new ground for the self in a form of being that satisfies its legitimate claims (indeed, civilization may be understood as an exercise in legitimating being). The civil savage has given up on the enterprise of justifying reality to the self, but affirms the condition of insufficiency from which that enterprise, religion and metaphysics, has arisen. As the most worldly of beings, he judges all fulfillments and satisfactions to be snatched from effort and struggle, and not to be intimations of a transcendent harmony, in which he already participates or might participate if only he oriented himself properly.

The most profound mark of fundamental adversity is the inherent division within the personal existent, the flesh-and-bone individual. When I look at life with an inward glance, pulling myself together in privileged moments of equilibrated alertness, I declare myself to be an individual, a dynamic integrity of streaming life-feeling. Yet almost immediately that unitary intuition falls apart into an uneasy and mutating suspension of spirit and flesh, observer and observed, or, in the terms of William James, "reflective ego" and "present acting self." It is not even altogether accurate to interpret the individual dualistically, since the flesh falls apart into a compound of body and psyche, the first experienced as an automatism and the second as a complex of impulse and feeling, centered in mood. Indeed, the individual is a trialistic, not a dualistic being, for whom awareness and corporeality are mediated by a heterogeneous and volatile connective tissue, the psyche, which is embedded in the diverse members of the body through sense and feeling, penetrates the ego through imagination and pacts between the two in what is variously termed attitude, disposition, and mood. The struggle of struggles is to integrate these diverse and often warring components into a dynamic order that makes it possible for the ego to affirm that life is worth living and that makes the individual an instrument for creating and appreciating the pleasures of the world. That is, for the civil savage, simply living is not a self-evident good: being is not on its face good, but he must make himself good enough to enjoy its pleasures wholeheartedly. Hedonism is the axiological consequence of living without transcendence, which means that the civil savage's existence is divided between preparing for pleasure and enjoying it. His deep sorrow is that much of life must be spent on defending it from internal breakdown and external threat, making the preparatory activities far more time-consuming than those of enjoyment. Far from making him desperate for pleasure, so as to redeem life from its ever-present torture, his recognition of the ubiquity of adversity tinges his mood with compassion, for himself and for all other conscious flesh.

Compassion grounds the life of defense, which reaches its relative perfection in the ideal of sanity, a just appreciation of all of the major dimensions of life and, most deeply, an acceptance of its failure ever to be reconciled to itself. The man of flesh and bone centers himself at the core of the psychic connective tissue, enveloping mood: his task, when he reaches self-lucidity as the civil savage, is the ruthlessly practical one of mood management. Discipline is the counterpoint of compassion and must always remain such because self-overcoming and self-perfection are inherently tenuous, and weakness eventually erodes gains and makes it necessary to renew the struggle. In Freudian terms, regression is a constant undercurrent in the victories we win to become adequate to the challenges that face us. The civil savage undertakes defensive life, the project of reversing declining vitality, in a mood or spirit of ruthless compassion. Each component of his sundered being must be worked over with a demanding love, according to its special requirements, so that he will be able to continue to achieve sanity, which is just that mood of ruthless compassion, the spirit through which the full range of experience is admitted to reflection appreciatively and then is manipulated and fashioned into a dynamic order directed toward the creation and enjoyment of goods. First, the spirit must be exercised and nurtured intellectually, by freeing it from as many prepossessions as possible, so that it can entertain any hypothesis imaginable; and then it must be trained to apply the various standards of evaluating knowledge that are the cognitive legacy of civilization. Thought must be made free: the sane mind is the one that tolerates any idea, and then judges its adequacy according to multiple criteria. Second, the body must be exercised and equilibrated, because, unlike the spirit, it is a determinate system of functions, each of which must be harmonized with the others to attain the transparency of health. Finally, the psyche must be interpreted by discerning the status of its warring desires through the various techniques of the different schools of psychoanalysis. Here, at the center of life, is also its irremediable irresolution: the psyche has no principle of perfection but the ability to enjoy, which is far more uncertain than the freedom of thought and the harmony of the organism. The crux of life is the clash between imagination and corporeality, of the possible and the actual, registered as overreaching and conflicting desire. The art of life is managing this strife.

There are many ways of characterizing the strife within personal existence, which is the fullest expression of being as we know it: the conscious flesh or the incarnated spirit, precariously unified by a complex of disparate emotions and feelings and centered in a point of observing and directing awareness, the ego. All of the time-honored ontological distinctions such as possibility and actuality, essence and existence, ideal and real, necessity and contingency, transcendence and immanence, and spirit and nature, are derived from the inward apprehension of our divided being and projected on the cosmos. Among its many functions, philosophy serves to remind us of the fissures and tensions within ourselves, which are usually available to reflection and are always incipient, since the processes of life's unmaking are in play even when vitality is ascending and experience appears to be reaching a consummation. The examined life borders its pleasures, which it embraces wholeheartedly, with an awareness of their transiency and an appreciation of the Hindu trinity of creation, preservation, and destruction: Brahma, Vishnu, and Shiva. Most often, however, it is not pleasure that obscures the war within us from our awareness, but the defensive posture itself, the practicality of the everyday round of affairs. Ordinary practical life is constituted by activity, getting something done. For the most part, we place ourselves, after periods of adjustment, in relatively stable niches where we are sufficiently competent to accomplish what must be done to perpetuate our design of living. The inherent structure of practicality is distance between present circumstance and some future desired state of affairs. In order to reach the desired future, it is necessary to work, not only in the sense of exerting physical effort, but also in the sense of applying the aesthetic and intellectual imaginations to tracing a course from here to there and now until then. Here is the wisdom of Freud's motto, ''work and love,'' the two primal commitments of personal existence meeting that which is other to itself: work is the defensive and love the erotic. When the daily round of affairs becomes sufficiently regularized, the distance between what is present and what remains to be accomplished almost seems to vanish in the process of achieving successive goals, and the imaginative seems to merge with the perceived, their difference vanishing at the point of habit. Habit, according to William James, is the "flywheel of civilization," practicality become natural rhythm. It is just this somnolence of action that is perpetually broken by failure, which opens up the gap between self and world, and the rift within the self.

Philosophy seizes upon failure in order to illuminate personal existence. The root of ontological distinctions is practicality and, beneath that, the self responding to adversity. As every child understands intimately, competence, most profoundly the control of one's own organic functions, is a hard-won achievement. The ideal is obviously not the real, the possible not the actual, and the necessary not the contingent for those who cannot control themselves from within and have not mastered the rudimentary skills required for routine participation in communal life. What of the aged, the infirm, and the mad? They know that the essence of life is Dionysian struggle, because society raises its requirements above the capabilities of the weak, at best providing special and usually dismal places for them to survive, and opening up a more generous opportunity structure for those who can take advantage of it. At bottom, strength is relative and weakness absolute. This is the lesson of all of the great world civilizations, which tends to be forgotten by those who have been bedazzled by the dream of self-sufficiency through technology. The civil savage grounds his life upon insight into its insufficiency, heeding the biblical wisdom that work is a curse: we are impractical beings who are doomed to practicality, and practical achievements are uncertain and tenuous.

Practicality is always breaking down. When I wake up and simply do not feel fit to respond adequately to the demands of the day, when I make a mistake or suffer an accident, when unforeseen circumstances derail my action, and when the probabilities work against me, I experience acutely the distance between present and desired situations. Ordinarily I do not stop to reflect upon what import this distance has for the structure of life. Instead, I alter my means, ends, or both, in a process of reciprocal adjustment, and plunge into activity once again. Sometimes, however, failure appears in such an extreme form that it is impossible for me to do anything but contemplate its revelation about my life. Then I grasp that defensive life is a process of throwing a net of judgments and interpretations proceeding from the imagination, over a present and stubbornly determinate perceptual reality. I am thinking here of a rare experience, which many people probably have not suffered for sufficient duration to recognize it, but of which I hope to provide some intimations.

Any time you make a mistake it is open for you to understand that your judgments of how things are have not been appropriate to the circumstances you confront. Now imagine that you have lost all certainty about the applicability of even your most elementary judgments about what lies beyond the perceptual awareness of the here and now; for example, you are walking down what should be a familiar street, but you suddenly find that you do not know where you are, that you do not know how to find your way home, though it is only a block away. You have lost spatial and temporal perspectives, which are the most primary of cognitive judgments, and which you take for granted as spontaneous guides to living beyond pure perceptual presence. A cognitive cripple, you are frozen in an intellectual panic, an epistemological psychosis: practicality has been deconstructed into its components of judgment and perception, the first the contribution of your own cogitating ego and the second the refractory other, which is just what it is, providing no guide within itself to what lies beyond it in space and time. Now possibility and actuality, necessity and contingency, and ideal and real are not general ideas about the nature of the cosmos but expressions of the frailty of the fleshly spirit. All you can do is to hold fast to actuality, to proceed into the unknown, walking without any confidence at all, meeting each actuality in its brute particularity, relying only on your body's spontaneous coordination and the equally spontaneous synthesis of sensation. You are fully cognizant of the inadequacy of your judgment, indeed, you may even confuse the present situation with memories of similar circumstances, knowing that you cannot trust these hypotheses. This is the existential counterpart of Descartes's methodical doubt, the concrete experience of skepticism. Existential skepticism is a privileged experience, dear to the civil savage, which teaches him more than any other how tenuous is his hold on life.

⇩

The experience of existential skepticism is the microcosmic confrontation of the personal existent with radical uncertainty. The theme of uncertainty dominated the thought of the pragmatists of the golden age of American philosophy. C. S. Peirce, William James, and John Dewey initiated their reflections by appealing to the experience of lived doubt in which the individual wrestles with a real problem, attempting to bring some action to a satisfactory conclusion. They opposed this actual, everyday doubting to Cartesian methodical doubting, which they criticized as a technical exercise divorced from life and resulting in abstraction. However, they failed to penetrate to the core of insecurity, the tense disjunction between perception and judgment, which is the root of our lack of confidence. American philosophy has been practical in the relatively superficial sense of searching for a resolution, within the world of finite things, of the torn self, a reconciliation of individual and world. Such a reconciliation, as Dewey recognized, presupposes an abandonment of the ''quest for certainty'' through which the self seeks to escape itself or to transcend itself to a ground that transfigures and transvalues the world. That is, the pragmatists proposed to deconstruct civilization and in their efforts helped to usher in the era of postcivilized life, without, however, understanding the consequence of their reflection, which was to expose the radical contingency within the depths of the individual, the provisional status of all of our judgments.

Among the American philosophers, only David Swenson, who attempted to synthesize Peirce's pragmatism and Kierkegaard's existentialism, came close to revealing radical contingency, in his notion of ''objective insecurity.''[2] For Swenson, we could never have sufficient assurance about the structure of things to achieve stable judgments about the world and our place in it. Relying at best upon probabilities, we had to admit, if we were self-lucid, that every choice in the here and now contains an irreducibly arbitrary element. Acceptance of arbitrariness meant that the final resource of the individual is not common sense or scientific and technical knowledge, but wholehearted or sincere commitment. Had Swenson taken one more step into the abyss of existential skepticism, he would have understood that an even deeper structure than objective insecurity is subjective insecurity, which divides the self from itself. Is it possible, after all, even to be sincere?

If my practical judgments are contingent, that is, if they have no necessary relation to what they purport to refer to, I am constitutively alienated from that which is other to that aspect of me that judges; I must always work to place myself in the world, which here includes my body and great stretches of my psyche. This fundamental alienation, which is expressed emotionally as anxiety, is remediated in everyday life by all of the acquirements of self-control and skill that create habit and routine, and that allow the individual to meet a more-or-less extended range of unforeseen events. Yet the limited activities of getting something done within my round of life do not exhaust my choices. There is a kind of work, done by the self upon itself, which does not fall easily under the reign of habit or skill or even under pragmatism's prized achievement—the intellectual imagination. Existential skepticism shows me that my judgments belong, finally, only to me, even if I have gained most of them through the social transmission of a culture, which results from the work of countless other individuals. I must, so long as I live, determine myself with regard to the world, decide who I am to be, and choose among my judgments, even to the extreme of deciding whether or not to be appropriate to my circumstances. It is paradoxical that as long as my practical life proceeds routinely and with relative success I am apt to believe that my judgments are reciprocal mediations rooted both in the world and in myself (real bridges), whereas when perception and judgment fall asunder, I claim my judgments as my own and am no longer alienated from them, though they may prove to be utterly untrustworthy. In the moment of severance I realize that I throw the bridge across the gulf between spirit and flesh, and that only sometimes does it catch hold on the other side. I imagine that schizophrenics face this epistemological predicament but that the schizophrenic psyche is too incoherent and has too many conflicting desires and, especially, fears, to tolerate it. So, they must project a set of judgments onto the world and maintain them there fixedly, even if they are grossly inappropriate. Postcivilized life, which is fabricated by the externalized imagination of the mass media of ''entertainment'' (the euphemism for a continuous failed therapeutic process), fosters a generalized cultural schizophrenia. Civil savages avoid cultural schizophrenia only by virtue of cultivating a free intellect, a harmonious body, and an examined psyche.

I must make some connection to the world; this is the grand presupposition of practicality become self-aware through acknowledgment of the contingency of judgment. Here, too, is the freedom of the civil savage: to build some sort of bridge to that which lies beyond himself. The perplexity of determining a connection to the world, which undercuts the question of who I am with the more radical problem of whom I will choose to be, appears most clearly to a life that has ascended sufficiently to find itself possessed of a vital surplus, an energy and capacity outrunning the requirements of the sheer survival of the flesh in its ecological niche and of the psyche in its network of social relations. Most human life in our times is still so embroiled in the struggle to survive physically and socially that it has not become aware of the possibility of deciding, day by day, how to dispose itself in the world, and of engineering a mood and temperament, of devising a self-conscious strategy for living. Increasingly, however, among the broad middle classes of the West, vast stretches of free time are appearing that beg to be filled with pursuits in order to ward off the terrible scourge of loneliness, which is rooted in the withering insight that each personal existent is superfluous. The genius of Jean-Paul Sartre was to connect the radical contingency of choice with the intimate awareness of the individual's superfluity: we are simply and most basically ''in the way'' of one another. How different this is from Aristotle's notion of leisure, which was based on the optimistic premise that the human being is a rational animal with potentialities that would, when satisfied, bring happiness in their wake. The rational animal has only to inquire into life and he will find out what is good for him. There is nothing that is necessarily good for the Sartrian ego, the legatee of the Pauline spirit, which is stripped of grace and along with it of any sense of an inward calling that would found a vocation, a necessary bridge to the world.

When the separation of judgment from perception is encountered *in extremis*, that is, in the moment of existential skepticism, the self is gripped by a terrible insecurity, that makes impossible any cool reflection on the structure of life but provides in compensation for that a direct insight into the components of human knowledge. There is also a more reflective experience of epistemic separation, which is macrocosmic and constitutes a way of being toward life that may prolong itself or be prolonged over hours, days, or even periods of a person's vital career. Since the mid-nineteenth century, a number of Western thinkers have found themselves in a state of suspension from action or of detachment from their own activity. Descartes, perhaps, experienced such detachment when he fell back upon himself as his object of inquiry, but he short-circuited the loneliness of the passive spirit, hovering above the flesh, by contemplating the idea of perfection that he had inherited from scholasticism and by connecting with the world through his provisional morality and his project of scientific inquiry. Others who followed his inward path embraced the moment of solitude and filled it with all of the appearances that they entertained, enjoying them as moments of consciousness and not as indicators of external realities. This is the technique of the ''eidetic reduction'' of phenomenology, which ''brackets'' any judgment about whether or not a conscious appearance evidences something independent of the consciousness of it, and simply observes that appearance.

Edmund Husserl attempted to make his reduction a method of inquiry into the ''essences'' of the objects of ''intentionality,'' but this effort to make work out of what really is aesthetic appreciation stands now as but an instance of trying to reclaim civilization when its foundations had already been undermined. Schopenhauer, who preceded Husserl by a century, had already discovered that the ego's suspension of worldliness primarily functioned to remove individuals from the clutches of the ''will to live'' by transporting them to an ethereal experience in which even anxiety is but the phenomenon of anxiety, to be contemplated rather than suffered or, more accurately, as it is suffered, thereby, as George Santayana said, relieving its ''sting.'' Santayana called the detachment from will the ''life of spirit'' and, as he grew older, he cultivated it as the consolation for being born. However, this is as much a short-circuiting of the loneliness of spirit as was Descartes's enjoyment of the idea of perfection, exploding the fetishism of a single thought into the fetishism of all appearances. It heals the scission of judgment and perception by fusing them in the specious present of consciousness.

Far more profound than the aesthetic turn, which has been the primary means of responding to spiritual detachment, was the quiet agony of the Swiss humanist Amiel, who recorded his anguish in voluminous diaries, which were published after his death. Amiel is the Protestant who is cut off from any call and, therefore, who must spend his life reviewing all of his options without ever daring to commit himself to any of them, a hesitation neurosis become existential. In his solitude Amiel felt his life slipping away from him as each day he performed his professional duties routinely and failed to endow any possibility with sufficient importance to claim his being. However, within the context of his desperate stagnation something very positive grew, an appreciation of the inward value quality of the religions and philosophies that human beings had constructed to give their lives orientation. Amiel, then, evinces the separation of judgment from perception when it bears upon the question of how to live. To the degree that he appreciated and understood all of the ways in which form could be given to life, he fell further away from being able to provide his own existence with any form other than the routine that he had achieved before he fell prey to his vocational crisis. He let his practical life live him while his personality remained without justification, the bitter end of the Protestant romance and the signal that the nerve of modern civilization had been cut. Amiel craved practical necessity, just as Descartes had, and found only contingency, which he could not tolerate.

The agony of Amiel, the detached ego searching for a reason to build a bridge to the world and finding that there is none, is the final spiritual moment of modern civilization, which is repeated over and over again in such formulations as Albert Camus's "absurd," Jean-Paul Sartre's "useless passion," and Martin Heidegger's "boredom." The agonizing undercurrent of the defensive side of life is the burden of freedom, the struggle to direct life when no necessity can be found to direct it in any particular way. No judgment about who I should be and what I should do carries sufficient emotional and intellectual insistency to compel me to take it seriously, so I fall into an irritated torpor, trying to minimize the demands upon myself to act, so that I can achieve peace, only to find peace disturbed by a wayward restlessness, carrying me to feel my organism intensely as I run over all of the things that I might be doing now and feel a numbing terror about all the things I will have to do in the future to survive. I am restlessly at rest, discontented with the success that I have had in bringing my life to the point at which I no longer have to do anything to maintain it for the moment: my vital surplus chokes me because I can find no proposition that suits me or that is adequate and appropriate to my vitality.

I call the suspension from will the "zero point" of life, the point at which I am left alone with my mutating flesh, without even the desire to desire, the wish to hear a call, or the hunger for diversion, yet with the residue of these, a primal irritability. This is the baseline condition of the civil savage, when everything is possible but nothing is necessary, when I am "doing nothing" and experience (drink to the dregs) my superfluity. I am free at the zero point and I glory in that freedom, because it is a purgation of all of the connections to the world that I have made, a revelation of the truth of the contingency of all of my judgments that bind me into the world. I seek out this restless repose when it does not befall me often enough, because it is the seedbed out of which ruthless compassion grows. I am not like Amiel; I have given up on the quest for justification. I shall not hear any call, but must fabricate my war cry out of the scraps of sensation and interpretation that perception and imagination offer me. If I never emerge from suspended detachment, I will be able to assent to the truth of my condition and to the knowledge of severance that it repeatedly imposes upon me. The ruthlessness of the judgment that everything is possible is balanced by the compassion that nothing is necessary, and at the zero point compassion is the victor, enveloping all of the guilt over letting life slip away and all of the pretension to self-importance.

The line of thought that leads out from Kant to our present mentality of postcivilized modernity has several strands, depending upon how thinkers have interpreted the balance between judgment and perception in the unsociable social being, the personal existent. The first of the post-Kantians, J. G. Fichte, grasped most fully the Kantian moment of modern individuality in his realization that the ego is not merely the Cartesian thinking substance but the seat of practical activity, a dynamic process of living-into the world, indeed, in a flight of metaphysical speculation, of constituting the world. He privileged judgment and the ego, making perception and inclination merely resistances to the ego's project of actualizing rational perfection. In contrast, Schopenhauer focused on inclination and desire, on gathering our manifold impulses into the will to live and holding judgment relative to that will, rendering the conscious self a passive reflector of the vicissitudes of vitality. From Fichte, thought proceeds to Max Stirner's ego, the "creative nothing" that seeks full possession of and discretion over the body in which it appears, and, finally, to Sartre's *pour soi*, the "nothingness" of consciousness that projects possibilities on a brutally actual world of determinate facts. Schopenhauer's legacy is taken up by Nietzsche through his notion of the will to power, and then by Georg Groddeck, who made the embodied psyche, what he called the "it" (Freud's "id"), the source of all of the ego's plans and reflections. In Sartre and Groddeck we find the Kantian system fragmented into the components that it had held in tension. For Groddeck we are lived by the corporeal-ized psyche, whereas for Sartre we create ourselves through our projects, which never satisfy our will to make the world our own; these are the two extreme interpretations of the struggle between spirit and flesh, the first giving way to the flesh in a manner similar to the Taoist's "doing nothingness," and the second ennobling the graceless spirit as frail master, the final irony of modern civilization deconstructing itself. The civil savage allows himself to experience both of these poles of experience, learning from them the lesson that he cannot reconcile himself to himself, that he need not relax into life with the compassionate Groddeck, or stand above it, directing it, with the ruthless Sartre, but may do either according to how he is moved by feeling or will, in an endless circle that he embraces.

At the zero point the civil savage witnesses the tensions of the lived body and reviews the incitements of possibility, embracing neither, yet privileging the flux of vitality by holding the self-conscious will to carry through any project in abeyance. He is somehow above life, while being immersed deeply within it, but is not beyond it, as the followers of the *Upanishads* strive, perhaps, to be. Vital suspension is a mediation between the active ego and the psyche's inclinations, in which each component checks the other, the ego neutralizing the insistency of desire and desire dissipating the seriousness of possibility: practical life is at a standstill. While the civil savage finds that he cannot deny the truth that everything is possible and nothing is necessary, he must also admit that there is something that is not final about the zero point. It is impossible, perhaps, really to be above life. Even in the moment of existential skepticism, when judgment and perception are severed, one is still embracing them both within an englobing field of lived experience, broken or impaired as it may be. Something is going on and is being created, even if it is only this peculiar vital suspension, which is not a pure stasis but has an irritable dynamic of its own. I am neither being lived by my corporeal psyche nor am I directing myself to accomplish a task, but I am experiencing both poles simultaneously in a manner that I cannot express in noncontradictory terms. I discover that I am, as Henri Bergson put it, a compound of mutually contradictory and compatible forces, a mysterious synthesis of life. And at the moment that I reach this recognition I am beyond the zero point, that is, beyond any temptation to harden the suspension of will into a fixed perspective as Husserl and Santayana did. I am ready to participate in being because I have found that I already do so, whether I like it or not. Everything is possible and nothing is necessary, but I am involved in a dynamic process, an activity: I am determinate in my indetermination; there is a necessity to my contingency.

Here I encounter the root out of which all of my further thinking and doing will grow, the gift of Islamic civilization: Hallaj's declaration-deed, ''I am the creative truth.'' As I say these words and seek to suffuse my being with them, I wonder how anyone ever could have doubted that subjectivity is real, could have thought that life might be a dream, could have had to retire into solitude in order to make himself an object of study and find something of which he could be certain. The great undeniable is that right here and now I am at the frontier of being, creating its truth through a synthesis of conscious will and of vitality, which seems in its depths to outrun my awareness of it. I do not mean that I embrace being in its totality, that I am cosmos or microcosmos, but that I am real, as real as anything can be and an actual creative dynamic. No being greater than myself can exclude me and I cannot be inadequate to such a greater being, because I am at least a genuine expression of that being, indeed, consubstantial with it, creating it as I receive it. This is a liberating and thoroughly democratic assent, which spells the end of alienation once it has been seized. It is the essence of arrogance and humility all at once, abolishing the distance between ideal and real at the same time that it maintains their tension by permitting them to struggle and to configure the creative process. The creative truths of fighting, loving, dying, ascending, and declining, all of these are being itself.

I am the *ens realissimum*, the most real of reals. I know of no greater and more fruitful thought than this, the harvest of philosophy. Yes, I am the most real of reals, because any greater reality is but an idea that appears within the truth that I am creating at this moment. Being is a democracy of experience and valuation is an incident within its flow rather than its structure or its rule. Being is not always good, but it always is, and I am one of its foci; more than a vice-gerent in the earth, I am a cocreator of the earth. I am so even as I waste away, because dissolution is itself a moment of being. To say that I am the creative truth gives me no guidance for practical life, since it carries me immediately beyond good and evil, but it provides me with something that is far more important, a firm standing in reality. Being is, in part, what it is because of me. What I am now indicates the actualization of a potential of reality, which means that it can never be judged by that reality, but only within it: being is not an authority that is detached from my present condition but is the affirmation of that condition. All divisions are relative to their appearance as creative truth. Of course, none of this takes away the truth of division, but only places it within a context of self-assurance. Is it not a wonderful gift to suffer radical insecurity with such confidence?

I proclaim that I am the creative truth with an overweening assurance, but I am also aware that it is not a logically demonstrable proposition or an hypothesis that can be verified by external perception. Indeed, it is a real assent, which is grounded in what Newman called "illation," or intellectual intuition, the most suspect of all of the ways of knowing. When it comes to real assents, it is necessary to admit that there might be many of them, in conflict with one another, and that each one can be negated, not only formally by its denial, but substantively by posing a meaningful alternative to it. So, even as I declare myself to be the creative truth and establish myself as such thereby (for it is the nature of a declaration-deed to create through the word), I am nagged and dogged by the small voice of doubt, questioning whether I have really accomplished anything. Must I not at least sympathize with the Taoist Chuang-Tze who, after awakening from dreaming that he was a butterfly, wondered whether he might now be a butterfly dreaming that it was the man Chuang-Tze? Indeed, I cannot refute Chuang-Tze, but perhaps his doubt does not touch my assurance radically. Whether the butterfly dreams the man or the man the butterfly makes no difference to the insight into creative truth, because in either case there is a conscious focus of creative process, some determinate actuality is in the process of formation. Yet in saying this have I not simply let go of the firm reality that I thought I had grasped, making my declaration-deed but a matter of appearance? By declaring myself to be creative truth I had affirmed my corporeality, my impulses, and my conscious volition to be real, and not the possible dream of a butterfly. There is no way out of the predicament. My intellectual imagination tells me that I might be the dream of some other being and my intellectual intuition responds that I do not, indeed, cannot, take that conceit or fancy seriously. I cannot get rid of the thought that I might be the appearance of a reality to which my consciousness has no access. So much for all of the hard-headed and consequently hard-hearted realism that has plagued late-modern civilization from Hegel through Marx to Freud, Dewey, and the contemporary gaggle of behaviorists, Leninists, ethologists, and cognitive scientists. There might be a Cartesian demon who deceives us about everything, including our own reality, a thought that Descartes could not tolerate. It does not help to say that we must live "as if" we were real and not a dream, because it is my reality that I seek to affirm. Indeed, I do not seek to affirm it; I assent to it more deeply than to anything else.

So I spin on a circular path, never achieving closure, but still firm in my infirmity and infirm in my firmness. Arrogant humility and humble arrogance: these are the consequences of my ruthless compassion when I face the limits of reason as I inquire into my being. I want more than the feeling of certainty that I am integral to being; I want to be sure that I am. I want my intellectual intuition that I am the creative truth to contain within itself the unshakable refutation of the counterthesis that I am but the appearance of an ulterior reality. Yet an intuition is not an argument, indeed, the clearer and more compelling it is, the more it refers only to itself and not to what contradicts it. I cannot have what I want and, thus, I suffer what Kant must have experienced when he ran up against reason's failure to resolve the traditional questions of ontology. Reason could not decide, for example, between the propositions that there was a first cause for events and that there is an infinite chain of events. Kant could only pit the two against each other, forming an irreconcilable antinomy. It seems that I can only do the same, counterposing the intuition of my reality to the imagination of my appearance. Even as I do this I find no comfort in the quietude of entertaining these two alternatives because they are not speculative hypotheses but summatory judgments on entire ways of living. I cannot achieve the certitude that I want, but I shall not hover above the antinomy, suspending judgment, since to do so would admit the distance and alienation that go along with believing that life is a dream. So, I shall hold steadfast to my intellectual intuition and border it with my doubt, circling arrogance with humility.

''Much ado about nothing,'' the linguistic therapist would say about all of my storming. ''Reality'' and ''being'' are perfectly fine words when they are used to fill places in the network of language, but not when they are abstracted from ordinary usage, which is always in the service of some intelligible pursuit, and injected into discourses that create problems without any conceivable solution. What difference could it possibly make to what I do day by day to believe that I am the creative truth? Could I not live the very same way and believe that I was an illusory appearance or a creature under God's direction? Perhaps it makes me feel better to believe that I am integral to reality or helps me better to achieve my specific goals. Others might find the matter to be different in their cases and be constituted so that they feel better believing that their experience is fantasy. Perhaps that belief gives them an ease in their actions and even makes them more practically effective because they are convinced that the results of what they do have no ultimate significance or even any importance at all. These perspectives on the status of the being of personal existence should be matters of personal choice because they have no cognitive import, but are ways of appreciating life and of providing it with greater impetus toward some fulfillment. As I listen to this voice of the postcivilized "specialist barbarian," as Ortega called him, I wonder who he takes himself to be.

I can only invite you to experience my intuition, which is not just a thought that I entertain and that entertains me, but a declaration-deed that permits me to become who I am by presenting my life to myself with the greatest lucidity that I am capable of achieving. Who is the "I" who uses the language? Just another word? I admit that I would not be fully myself if I could not express myself to myself in language, but I also cannot be myself without breathing every several seconds. I acknowledge my radical dependency upon that which is not the conscious focus of creating truth, but I seize that conscious focus as the core of my being, uniquely differentiated from anything that it intends. I do not know whether it is an emergent from more thinglike forms of being or whether it is always incipient throughout being; I only know that when I declare myself to be the creative truth, I am more radically individualized and yet more coincident than at any other instant with that which is not myself. It seems to me that the alternative to declaring myself to be the creative truth in postcivilized technological culture is to designate myself a functional element of a cultural system—to say, for example, "language speaks me." Has language, indeed, triumphed in its thousands-of-years struggle with human beings when it finally gets some speakers to declare it in this way? This absurdity is only one instance of a far more general culture worship that seeps into the mind when the power of civilization to individualize has been lost.

The discourse on civilization ends with the affirmation of the finitude of life and of the immanence of awareness to that life. The modern process has been one of demystification and, therefore, of increasing lucidity. All of the great world civilizations are now open to be plundered for whatever they have to offer to the unillusioned individual, who seeks in them invitations to experience the truths of his condition. The negative moment of criticizing all of the attempts to achieve transcendence is the ascetic discipline that is necessary for placing the individual in a position in which he can defend himself from an irrelevance or inappropriateness to his circumstances.

The defensive side of life, when it is brought to perfection, is a struggle to understand the truth of being and then to maintain a conscious grip on that truth tenaciously. There are all sorts of practical arts and social techniques that allow one to fend off threats and to gather strength, adaptability, and capability, but they are of no use unless one has the will to apply them to a clarified situation. The deep wish of the civil savage is to want to live in truth, not simply to live in truth, because the truth of being is excruciatingly uncomfortable when one's life is in decline and often acutely irritating when one is ascending toward a pleasurable fulfillment. The civil savage wants to be strong enough to embrace the will to power in its purity without any gloss of a vital lie, a carrot-stick of thought, what Nikos Kazantzakis called a "gum drop," which sweetens vitality and inspires it to grasp at alluring possibilities. Why should he hold steadfastly to the vision of a disenchanted world, the essence of modern wisdom, when it might be possible to convince himself to hope for something more attractive? Why should he embrace immanence when the lesson of every civilization has been that the spirit craves transcendence? If he is really serious about stemming life's decline and encouraging its advance, should he not distort his thought, if necessary, to make it productive of the unification and integrity of vital force?

Nietzsche's answer to these questions was that we think in order to live, and, therefore, that we should choose those thoughts to live by that enhance our vitality. This decision of his was the root of his madness, the cognitive or epistemic dimension of his psychosis, a prescription for projection. Postcivilized modernity is now going mad from its addiction to vital lies, which is why Nietzsche is the philosopher of our times. The civil savage's way is resistance to contemporary madness and has nothing, finally, to offer in its favor but sanity: one must learn to love sanity to understand the civil savage.

The presupposition of the defensive side of life is the struggle against madness, against projecting one's hopes and fears on the environing world. When I declare the radical immanence of my personal existence by proclaiming, in the light of doubt, that I am the creative truth, I do not establish a new ground for hope, but merely assure myself that I am real, which means that I cannot reinterpret anything that I do and experience as somehow less endowed with being than something else that I might imagine to be better or more noble. When I acknowledge at the zero point that everything is possible and nothing is necessary, I do not thereby free myself to enter into a transmundane reality, but simply admit my radical contingency and superfluity: I do not have to do anything in particular because the world does not need me, and I am not made or destined for anything special. When I suffer the disjunction of judgment and perception, in a wrenching moment of the decomposition of spirit and flesh, I do not gain admittance to the realm of Platonic forms, but confront the fundamental frailty of my being. These attitudes, intuitions, and experiences are the fruits of the demystifying process of modernity, what might best be called ''truth moods,'' and they provide me with the basis for sanity, with the grounds for a measured and appreciative judgment of the goods that the world has to offer. Together they form a democratic vision of being, that is expressed emotionally as ruthless compassion, because there is an inherent sadness to lucidity about the defensive side of life. To accept the disenchantment of the world is not to adopt a nihilistic pose, but to feel the sadness of having to fight to secure oneself tenuously over and over again within one's immanence and finitude.

The civil savage repudiates the transcendental pragmatism of the vital lie in favor of an inward glance at an unencumbered yet tortured personal existence. The theory of practice has as its first premise that I am an impractical being who is destined to work perpetually, even if I do not exert self-conscious direction over my projects and their execution. With assent to this premise comes the positive moment of the inquest into civilization, the plunder of its treasures: all of the insights that deepen appreciative awareness of the potentialities and possibilities of finite personal existence. The civil savage performs a deconstruction of civilization in order to disengage the wisdom that it can give finite life from its reference to a transcendent ground. In the pursuit of clarifying personal existence, he is a militant antipragmatist who is committed to exploring his being, wherever the expedition may lead him; in the terms of Dostoevsky's legend of the Grand Inquisitor, he chooses freedom over meaning, the freedom of the intellect to search out the regions of the domain of self-reference. Consequently, he discovers in his quest that his foremost problem is to marshal his will to take initiative over his life, because there is nothing external to that will that provides him with a self-evident incentive to be practical. In contrast to those who are addicted to a vital lie, he does not live through an inspiring idea, but gathers up the stirrings of vitality and of desire, and works them up ruthlessly into a life strategy, because one of the truths that he wants to live is that of life's finite integrity.

Clarity and lucidity about life are the criteria of the civil savage's self-inquest, but he is a radical pragmatist when he makes the decision to take initiative, to direct himself and to find out how much unity and

intensity he can bring to his vital powers, how many positive and mutually reinforcing connections he can make with the world. The defensive
side of life does not provide any reason for its being or any claim upon
the self, but is fulfilled only by passing over to the erotic side of life,
the appreciative union (spiritual, psychic, and/or physical) with that
which is other than the self. The positive connection of erotic union, in
the generous and comprehensive sense that Plato and Freud understood
the erotic, occurs only sporadically if its cultivation is left to the spontaneous processes of undisciplined life. The clarification of life confronted with adversity prepares individuals to enjoy for their own sake
the pleasures of the world, but does not fit them to achieve these pleasures. In order to achieve such fitness it is necessary to reorient thought,
shifting the tone of defensive life from the theme of compassion to that
of ruthlessness.

It is at this point that my free meditation reaches its watershed. Without any more reason than the promptings of vitality and the wish to
experience life ascend, I pass over from contemplation to the self-
conscious disposition of my personal existence in the world, carrying
with me what I have learned about my frailty.

Postcivilized life is harsh, uncompromising, and demanding in its
requirements for a thought that is adequate to it. In his abandonment of
the thought of transcendence, the civil savage does not return to the
world from his inward contemplation with a new bridge to the other,
but must look to that world itself for the materials to make his connection, to span the gulf that separates him from those who surround him.
As he inspects the society in which he dwells, he undertakes first an
epistemological reflection on the prevalent forms of thinking, because
these will give him his purchase on externality and will show him how
to reorient himself and take initiative.

The characteristic form of thinking in postcivilized modern society
is functional thought; it is the specification of procedures for getting
something done within a complex system of activities a kind of how-to
knowledge and the essence of practicality. I do not claim that contemporary society has for its principle ''instrumental rationality,'' as the
line of thinkers from Max Weber through Talcott Parsons to Jurgen
Habermas have asserted. It is far too optimistic to claim that organized
social life is geared to the efficient use of means to achieve whatever

ends have been established by the ruling powers; it is sufficient to note a preoccupation with how to get results, whether or not the effort is effective, or even whether or not it succeeds. Technical thought far outruns the norms of engineering and of economic rationality, often lapsing into ritualism and fetishism, and, indeed, into a magic that is declared to be rational by its practitioners. The singular characteristic of contemporary thought is the understanding of thought as a function within life, an incident within a greater process that performs the role of moving experience from one point to another; that is, contemporary thought assents to the immanence of thought to life but refrains from clarifying life in favor of moving it along toward a series of ever-shifting goals. Thus, the civil savage finds himself to be well adapted to his epistemic environment and differs from his uncivil brethren only in carrying the immanence of thought to life inside himself with critical awareness. If he found around him a concern with the form of thinking that evaluates goods and places them in hierarchies, or with that which strives to transcend the self to an ulterior ground of being, or even with that which tries to understand the patterns through which things actually change, he would have suffered a social alienation in addition to the ruptures within himself. Instead, he sees that he is more at home in the world than those who have never detached themselves from it, because he has made himself thoroughly worldly.

Functional thinking, indeed, does not reach its postcivilized climax in physical, biological, or social technology, but in psychological technique through which the ego treats its experience as an object and tries to refashion itself into an image of itself that will please itself. The underlying form of work today is labor upon the self, undertaken in order to create the personality as a consumer good to be enjoyed in private contemplation and as a commodity to be marketed for the return of institutional security and advancement, and, perhaps more importantly, to acquire positive reinforcement of itself from others. The goal of goals in postcivilized society is to "feel good about oneself," and, hence, its most preferred form of thinking is the vital lie, whichever lie seems to be satisfying and expedient at the moment.

Nietzsche is the ruler of the postcivilized world, his desperate attempt to escape the truth of life having been appropriated and absorbed by declining life, not to achieve some measure of nobility but to entertain transient pleasing feelings. Since the touchstone of success is a feeling, a self-feeling devoid of objectivity, the characteristic setting of functional thought is the entertainment industry, which provides images for individuals to introject and, therefore, to define themselves. This is the culmination of Marshall McLuhan's "global village," the anticommunity of non-civil savages manipulating the products of a vast externalized imagination, contrived by their own kind and not by a Grand Inquisitor who stands apart from them by virtue of his existential agony. The noncivil savage is not a worldly being but rather has become a fully encultured organism.

The civil savage is at home with his noncivil brethren: let us call them once and for all uncivil, because they have no understanding of what civilization was, and are incapable of plundering its treasures. He understands them deeply because he knows the temptations of the vital lie to the lonely ego, suspended in isolation with no exit to transcendence. What a simple move of thought it seems to be to push psyche, body, and even judgment away from the ego and to treat them as objects to be fashioned to procure comfort, or as instruments to feeling. The civil savage can see through the pacts that others have made with themselves and responds to them with compassion. Yet what a price it is to pay to exist within the incitements of the externalized imagination and to use them as excuses to implode the objective world into oneself. The civil savage responds to the ubiquitous psychoses around him with a ruthless rejection of the mad dance of "I'm OK, you're OK," which they require for their maintenance. The mass media of entertainment signal the normalcy of a schizophrenia that rests upon the epistemic reference to pure self-feeling, the final justification of all functional thinking when it loses a prior clarified reference to objectivity. The new jungle, savannah, desert, and tundra are the cultural zones of mass-mediated life. The civil savage maps them and then seeks objective reference beyond them.

The civil savage embraces functional thinking wholeheartedly, but not that extension of it into self-formation through the vital lie. Instead, he absorbs that most troubling of the moderns, Lenin, into himself and transforms philosophy of conduct into the reflection on life strategy. Everything practical is a matter of strategy and tactics, of "what is to be done" to "smash the state" of postcivilized culture (the externalized mind), clear away its ruins, and create an internal order of intellectual imagination that is capable of leading the individual into the world to enjoy its difficult pleasures, the goods that demand effort, training, sagacity, and mutuality, while keeping him away from the "good" of feeling good about himself, which is the greatest threat to sanity and the fluid in which so many lives are dissolved. Life for the civil savage is worth living only because there are finite goods to be enjoyed by going out into the world and connecting with other, independent realities, which and who have their own integrities that must be honored to appreciate them and not merely to esteem oneself through them. The essence of life strategy is the process of mobilizing the compound of spirit, psyche, and body to throw a bridge across the gulf separating self and world, a process of self-rule and not of the fabrication of self-image.

The struggle to love the world for its goods is the *telos* of the practical life for the civil savage, who lives in the world for the world and not for something lying beyond the finite and mundane. He is the nonalienated counterpart of the uncivil savage, whose alienation arises from existing in a self-reflexive and functional order of social organizations that have no reference to transcendence. These uncivil savages are unwilling or unable to tolerate the disenchantment indicated by everyday life, and, therefore, seize upon any images in their cultural environment that inflate their self-feeling. Such people have grasped one of the prime possibilities of a technological order: to free the vital surplus expressed in appreciative subjectivity from any integral connection to its concrete circumstances. Accordingly, the television mystic is the representative personality of our time. His god is the celebrity; indeed, even the God of Jerusalem becomes a sort of celebrity in the "electronic church."

It is a grievous mistake to believe that the appearance of hordes of uncivil savages participating in an externalized imagination indicates the emergence of a narcissism that should be criticized sternly in the manner of a parent scolding some spoiled child. The retreat into self-feeling is the intelligible consequence of the destruction of civilization, which leaves individuals, whether they like it or not, in the predicament of having to find incentives for continuing to maintain their fragile integrities against internal dissolution and external threat. It is simply difficult to live under any circumstances, and the self must ceaselessly strive to establish itself securely against the eroding processes of declining life.

If a vast system of inciting images has been contrived to placate the unresolved and suffering will, the civil savage can only accept it as the way in which life has, proximally and for the most part, adapted to the predicament of continuing its own course. He must live within this variegated cultural doubling of nature, participating in it enough to map it and to read its signs, but only so that he can discover its rents and fissures, and dwell in its interstices where a more direct contact with the stream of creative process can be made. The uncivil savage is still seeking salvation, the gift of the Pauline holy spirit, and he finds it in the imaginative contrivances of his own kind. This is the triumph of the fetishism that was cursed more than anything else by all of the religions of Jerusalem, the worship of one's own creations, which is the last result of life's desperation. The civil savage, having given up on saving grace from any quarter, must encounter in another way the desperation of being an impractical being, fated to practicality. He must take control of his imagination and become its ruler.

"I am the creative truth" is the intellectual intuition that founds the civil savage's orientation to life. Yet this liberating declaration-deed is but a permission to engage oneself in a creative process in any manner that one chooses. Beyond the zero point at which everything is possible and nothing is necessary is the decision to direct self-consciously one's connection to the other-than-self. This decision is fateful because it must be undertaken radically. With no exit to transcendence but possessed of the treasures of the world civilizations, I shift the position of the ego within my orientation and make a new declaration: "I am the God of myself." Suddenly I am in potential command of the domain of my subjectivity, which is composed of my desires and fears. I can do anything with them that I wish as long as I am strong enough to hold fast to them in all of their variety and mutual tension, and then to let none of them usurp my control over their expression and release. The field of desire is my realm and it is not simply a kingdom of felt impulse but, far more importantly, one of imagination. My dreams that appear in the night world of sleep and my fantasies that intrude upon the day world of wakefulness are the substance of the community of my psyche, each figure in them a personification or symbolization of some desire or fear.

Here is where my struggle begins and ends, in the psyche, which gives me my independence from the externalized imagination of the mass-mediated culture and which provides me with my own incitements for throwing a bridge to the other. My self-generated, spontaneous imagination is a tribe; I am a tribal being that has for its potential ruler the ego: "I am the God of my tribe," my own Yahweh, and I must learn how to command.

The overriding principle of self-rule is that the members of my tribe, the inhabitants of dream and fantasy, including my own shifting self-images, are my faithful. I do not worship them nor do I worship myself (I am no more worshipful than is the God of Jerusalem), but I command and protect, discipline and love them, and I tenaciously hold my position of direction. I know of no more perfect description of the art of rule than the *Koran*: ''I am Allah to myself.'' The God of Jerusalem, as portrayed in the *Koran*, asks from the faithful only submission to God's majesty and, after that, God is willing to accept their lapses into weakness and imperfection, requiring no more than what they are capable of doing in their frail condition of clay infused with a drop of water, the conscious mind. God issues the plain warning and reminder that the disloyal will be punished and that the loyal will be rewarded, and, most importantly, God is merciful. The spirit of Allah is ruthless compassion, the thorough acknowledgment of adversity and the need to struggle against it, and the even greater tolerance of failure. I shall treat myself this way, limiting any desire or fear that seeks to dislodge me from self-command and rewarding those that help me connect to the world so that I enjoy the goods that are available in it. I shall set these desires and fears free to explore the world and to respond to it, because their personifications in my imagination will interpret its goods and evils for me.

There is no meaning to life except what my desires and fears show me that the world contains. The ego has no content of its own but the ability to direct, inhibit, and encourage impulse. Out of the thousands of incitements to action my work must be to create an ever-changing integrity, a militant community whose members are eager and fit to engage the world and to plunder it appreciatively for its treasures. Within that community I must be Machiavelli's Prince, the conserving lion and the innovative fox, keeping the wolves at bay, preparing for war, allowing my charges to be themselves, and protecting them, as much as I can, from attack from the outside and from internecine war. I also must be Lenin, leading my tribe into the world, admonishing it to abandon the infantilism of impossible dreams and the revisionism of fearful withdrawal from change, and inspiring it to smash the enslaving state of postcivilized culture. I am the civil savage, expelled from Eden and on my own, barefoot on a beach cluttered with the shards of civilization, dancing with a bitter olive in my mouth: I am Nietzsche chastened and sane, willing to be sad and to pity, ready to embrace the pleasures of the world. Freed of hatred, but filled with a healthy scorn of illusion, I go out to fight the war for pleasure.

⇩

Chapter 3

Erotic Life

The civil savage is the heir to the legacy of all of the reflections on the meaning and prospects of life that were undertaken by the creators and the sustainers of modern civilization. Life became a genuine problem, indeed, an agony, for the modern spirit when it was made its own object of inquest in the first half of the nineteenth century, particularly in the demystifying thought of Schopenhauer and Giacomo Leopardi. Grasping their own experience from within and holding fast to it, the two great pessimists of the romantic period discovered that the daily round of engagements in the world provided no ready incentives to continue the struggle to persist in personal existence.

For Schopenhauer, the will of the world, expressed within each individual as desire, was insatiable and deceitful, holding out the prospect of authentic satisfaction in the imagination, but humiliating enthusiasm in the inadequacy of actual achievement. The cycle of ordinary life had the form of a repetition neurosis or, perhaps, of a manic-depressive psychosis, in which excessive lust was inevitably succeeded by frustration only to emerge again to draw the self outside itself into new phantasms. Acknowledgment of the failed structure of life led Schopenhauer to boredom, the desire to desire neutralized by the expectation of futility, the mood of the ''window gazer'' who contemplates exterior life with stale feeling, or of today's television viewers staring through their electronic windows. Schopenhauer was an early explorer of vital surplus, having remarked that the profounder tortures of life begin only after a person has temporarily met the requirements of survival and faces head-on the perplexity of what to do next. Then it becomes apparent that there is no object of will that is capable of slaking its thirst, no peace even after the fulfillment of organic need. Confronting this situation, Schopenhauer tried to renounce the will to live and to lose himself

in moments of aesthetic contemplation in which experience is transiently carried beyond the gap between desire and object; he was the
prophet of television with a private video of the imagination.

Leopardi, similarly, traveled the deserts of disillusioned life, having
understood that human beings desire happiness but can form no coherent conception of it as an attainable goal. His truth mood was *noia*, an
overpowering sense of spiritual exhaustion, a reflective ennui at the very
edge of a sweet acceptance of life's constitutive inadequacy to its native
demand. Yet no more than Schopenhauer could Leopardi embrace the
world, which was not good enough for the will. They were transcendental utilitarians who touched the limit of, and then passed beyond, the
practical hedonism of the industrial revolution.

Pessimism founds the modern philosophy of life and poses as its
primary concern the affirmation of the world. Ever since the appearance
of romantic pessimism, the modern spirit has battled to establish some
grounds for optimism; its failure to succeed signals the onset of the
post-civilized era in which the category of transcendence is obliterated.
As classical philosophers of life, Schopenhauer and Leopardi attempted
to totalize human existence, to specify its purposive dynamic as a
whole, and, therefore, to integrate all of the particular desires within
that dynamism; that is, they performed a transcendental critique on life
similar to that which Kant had executed on natural science and Christian morality. In seeking its formative structure or principle, they found
that life was unreconciled within itself, that it was, in Santayana's
terms, in vital self-contradiction: there was no principle but only a useless, indeed, a pernicious passion, an ever-overreaching will or an incoherent wish. Modern optimism counterposed to this discovery a prolif-
eration of historical myths of progress and human perfectibility, but
none of them could speak to the condition of the separate self confronting its own existence. Instead they offered renunciation of present life
in favor of some future perfection, making care of the self for its own
sake a pathology.

For the civil savage, the judgment of the pessimists over life stands.
He wonders whether any future life could have essential differences
from his own. Individual life is, on the whole, a losing proposition, but
it is the only end in itself. The failed and frustrated flesh is its own
excuse for being or there is no reason for being at all. The civil savage
undertakes the war for pleasure in light of the revelations of pessimistic
philosophy of life. There is no effective neutrality in the debate between
optimists and pessimists, but only a choice between forthright and con-
cealed partisanship. The decision, however, is not arbitrary. I am not

concerned here with the problem of affirming life, which so occupied Nietzsche, who was the most clear-sighted, radical, and lucid of the optimists. I settle that issue not by a heroism that tests my commitment against the standard of eternal recurrence, but simply by a rather humble acknowledgment that vitality ascends and declines, and that so long as I feel sufficient vital promptings and urges to hurl myself forward, I shall do so, realizing that at some time I will be overwhelmed. That is, I do not seek to affirm all life but only my life here and now, day by day.

The mistake of the classical pessimists was not in their description of life. I can only invite you to take your inwardness seriously, to cherish it and not to embellish it with hopes and fears of things beyond its mundane deliverances; then I suspect that you will agree that you are too great for the world in your demands and too small for it in your powers. That is the core insight of classical pessimism, and all you must do to grasp and appreciate it is to take yourself seriously, though I do not deny how difficult it is to do that. The classical pessimists erred in their response to their discovery, which was to privilege overall failure and to deprecate partial success. They made of the zero point not a purgation but a life strategy, thereby demeaning erotic connection to the world, the other-than-self, because it could never offer sufficient satisfaction. The real task of philosophy of conduct is to affirm the world, to avoid suspension in the imagination, despite its allure, and to love the other-than-self without recourse to heroism.

Love the pleasures of the world: that is the civil savage's imperative for the erotic side of life. Love those pleasures, the delights that the other-than-self offers on its own terms, in full awareness that they can never be fully satisfactory and that they are not necessary. In this vein they will delight just for what they are and they will not deceive: they will be honored, even cherished, but not worshipped and made fetishes. Desire will still outrun fulfillment, adversity will still loom beyond potency, and life will often take on a bland, stale, and irritating tone, but pessimism will no longer debilitate because the nerve of nostalgia for transcendence will have been cut. That was the raw, exposed nerve that anguished Schopenhauer and Leopardi, a pining over loss, a grief, and, perhaps, a guilt.

I am civil because I feast upon the fruits of modern reflection, the truth that life revealed to it, and I am savage because I will find a way of loving what is lovely. This is why I so ruthlessly practice the arts of defense: train my body, cultivate my intellect, and most of all, mobilize my psyche. I strive to capture pleasure, to honor the world into which I have been thrown by enjoying it for its delights as they actually appear in themselves; I will, of course, have to seduce and coax them and continually make myself fit to relish them. The civil savage is an erotic hedonist.

Erotic hedonism is the civil savage's life strategy. As such, it is not offered as a proposition to demonstrate or as a virtue to practice, but as a program to consider and then to apply at will, in part or whole, to living. An answer to the question of ''what is to be done'' (what Ortega called an ''I-program'') is very personal and circumstantial. It is the complex and composite result of organs, habits, and specific virtues; it is what all of these are employed to accomplish. There is no universality to a life strategy, but when one is clarified and put into general terms, it can become fit for appropriation by others than its author.

I proffer erotic hedonism as a set of ways to lead a good life in post-civilized modernity. I am aware that both components of the strategy, the erotic and the hedonistic, will meet with resistance and misunder-standing in a society that, I believe, suffers from a severe case of anhedonia.

Eroticism is not meant here to apply specifically to sex, but is defined vitalistically, in Freud's fashion, as valued union with the other: to love the other is to unite with the other. The civil savage places restrictions on such union. The other is to be honored even when it is, at the fre-quently reached limit, consumed. Being honored endows the pleasure-giving others with dignity; not the dignity with which Heidegger sought to endow Being, but the dignity of good things. A fast-and-loose rever-ence for the sources of pleasure, coupled with an acute awareness of their dangers and limitations, is the closest that the erotic hedonist gets to religion—an ironic reverence. The civil savage is not a possessive individualist, a ''yuppie'' with an agenda, but a lover of particular oth-ers who does not exclude the possibility of abrogating hedonism in the name of sacrifice for the good of the beloved. The love comes first, but the fruition or fulfillment of love is pleasure.

As hedonist the civil savage assents to Santayana's apothegm: ''The only cure for birth and death is to enjoy the interval.'' There are multi-tudes of enjoyments, of heterogeneous pleasures, satisfactions, and joys offered by the world to someone with a vital surplus. The civil savage delights in the plurality of pleasurable unions, rejecting any effort to reduce them to some common denominator called pleasure, a feeling void of connection with its provider, some ultimate, purely subjective state detached from the world. Yet while embracing the heterogeneity of pleasures, the erotic hedonist retains a special connection to the sexual sense of eroticism (making love), which is for him the paradigmatic case of pleasurable union that when brought to perfection fuses honoring and consuming in a single act.

Now let me enter the dream of ethical discourse as it has developed in modern times, at least so far as my free meditation will permit me to do so. One of the great ironies of contemporary thought is that the subject that should produce the greatest delight for reflection, the character of and possibilities for goodness, has produced a vast array of abstract and uninspiring technical discussions ranged under the heading of "ethical theory." The lack of joy in moral philosophy can be traced to Kant, who attempted to place ethics on a scientific footing and to show that the norm of conduct is a rational principle that can be considered in isolation from the concrete lives of individuals, apart from their existential struggles and their particular fulfillments in momentary experience. The idea that the moral philosopher should focus on prescription has turned the study of ethics into an effort to imagine a properly constituted society rather than an attempt to invite flesh-and-blood persons to experience their lives more intensely and richly. In the process, morality has been depersonalized, indeed, dehumanized, and has catered to the requirements of institutional functioning.

I do not doubt that the reduction of ethics to a concern of social organization has an intelligible basis in modern life. The rise of capitalism, industrialization, and democracy created a situation in which human relations had to be reconstituted in more general terms, relieved of the specific shadings of localism and tradition. The abstraction of the modern cosmopolis, its reliance on idealized plans that must be fulfilled by disciplined cooperation, leads to the fantasy that collaboration might proceed on the basis of a harmony of inward initiatives rather than through external constraints. Yet the very dream of voluntary solidarity becomes a coercive nightmare when attempts are made to describe how it should work in specific institutional contexts such as hospitals, business firms, and governmental agencies. Who merits receiving an organ transplant? How should the claims of shareholders be reconciled with a conception of the public interest? How responsive should the state be to shifting majority preferences? All of these questions and the many others that perplex contemporary moral philosophers result from the brute fact that modern society is not an integrated totality, but a field in which various human desires find partial organizational expression and then must be imperfectly composed into transient unities. As a consequence, the dialectics of reconciliation become a technical specialization, concealing and legitimizing sectoral interests in terms of notions of utility, freedom, and reason.

The civil savage has given up on the project of creating an ethic that is rooted in social organization. He moves back a step to the ethical concerns of the premodern civilizations, which centered on how the individual might lead a good life, because he has concluded that no principle can constitute a social totality in an impersonal technological order. The work of the ethical technicians will go on because there is an objective collective need to match private utility to public form, but the problem will not be resolved unless the old Adam is transformed into a new being who gladly submits to social role, a ''new socialist man'' or, more radically, a bionically engineered organism. Let the technicians labor over balancing lists of personal goods against general conceptions of justice, so that members of boards of directors of various organizations will not feel the sting of individual responsibility when they impose sacrifices. Let the rest of us be free to direct our attention to our own lives so that we can begin to discern what satisfactions the world offers us here and now. Ethical theory has been detached from personal life and has effaced pleasure and goodness, which have been left to a purely subjective determination, held inferior to justice. Yet to raise justice above individually achieved good is to invert the order of concrete life in which social arrangements are means to the consummations of personal experience that arise when activity forges satisfying connections to the world. The long road to a coherent society winds through the labyrinth of the self, heading toward love of the world, and it is the high road. Does it matter that it will never be traversed to its end?

The great distinction that an ethic that is close to life must make is between good and evil. I am far more clear about what I mean by evil than I am about my interpretation of goodness. Evil is adversity in whatever form it takes; that is, threat, attack, obstruction, decline, and dispersion, and their subjective resolutions, pain and suffering. Life is a losing proposition because it is shot through with so much evil, and it does not matter to me that adversity is often the occasion for efforts that achieve pleasures that might not have been enjoyed but for the ingenuity and tenacity wrested from struggle. I enjoy the goods that I win through striving without reducing the evil that impelled my overcoming to a necessary phase preceding fulfillment: the civil savage does not practice theodicy. In my rejection of theodicy, I encounter sin, not as rebellion against the commandments of God or the law of nature, but as acceptance, as embrace, of adversity within myself, as collaboration with and participation in evil: hatred of existence, life, and the world. It is so easy to hate existence and to give way to declining life, that I feel a deep sympathy with Nietzsche's battle against resentment, which drove him to madness. I am tempted to believe that goodness is no more than the triumph over evil, that not hating may exhaust the meaning of living well. At least the absence of hatred is the presupposition of goodness, the ground of its possibility and the clearest field upon which joy and delight may be constituted.

So I realize that I have worked beyond a merely negative conception of goodness by unavoidably saying the words joy and delight. Erotic hedonism is the name for the life that joys in the delights of the world, which cherishes and relishes the pleasures that the other-than-self offers to the self. This is not the classical hedonism that encloses the self within itself to experience private pleasures, nor is it the utilitarian hedonism that exploits the world as a stimulus to feeling, nor is it the Epicurean hedonism that tries to confine connections to the safety of the private garden, nor is it even the romantic hedonism that seeks to fuse with the world in Dionysian ecstasy. It is connection that loves the other as other and, therefore, holds fast to the self as self. However, though the core of goodness is delight in the pleasure-provoking other, I must also count as good all of the vitality that helps me to overcome evil, in its physical, emotional, and intellectual forms. Let me call that directed and struggling vitality of will, which allows me to bring myself and the other to the moment of enjoyment and to a finite perfection, virtue. Let me also call the full experience of delighting and enjoying, which embraces activity in all of its dimensions, pleasure. The good, then, is virtue in the service of pleasure and pleasure as the spur to virtue. I make contact with the contemporary ethical discourse through a theory of pleasure. What else but such a theory can satisfy the civil savage intellectually? I think of Socrates in the technological jungle, erotic philosophy restored.

The great problem for the unillusioned life is to come to terms with the world. The revival of philosophy of conduct in the nineteenth century signaled the dawn of what Jean-Paul Sartre called the "age of reason,'' the era in which self-reflective individuals could no longer resort to a notion of transcendent reality, beyond mutating appearance, to secure their purposes and, more importantly, their attitude toward existence. To be thoroughly modern is, as the critic Irving Babbitt held, to reject any external authority over the conduct of one's life and yet to seek through one's imagination a standard in terms of which to participate in the everyday round of affairs.

Modern philosophy of life is determined between the poles of rejection of the world, which is defined by Schopenhauer's pessimism, and its affirmation, which is most clearly proclaimed by Nietzsche's optimism. Confronting a horizon that lacks transcendence involves a harsh discipline of the self's separation from that which is other than itself, attended by the forms of self-criticism prefigured in premodern civilizations. The Taoist deprecation of self-importance, the Hindu reflection on the limitation of desire, the Islamic insight into constitutive anxiety, the Socratic strictures against regnant opinion, and the Pauline encounter with enfleshed passion all lead to the single acknowledgment by the self of its radical inadequacy to its own condition, a humbling recognition that eventually carries the self to take its own persistence and the gratification of its will lightly. In the absence of transcendence, the insufficient self, aware of its incessant frustration, can only look to the world for an incentive to continue the labor of living.

At the moment of disillusionment, nothing is more appealing than to follow Schopenhauer's counsel of world rejection. Yet the prospect of rejecting the world is agonizing for the civil savage. He understands that the very essence of civilization is to provide the self with a compensation for or at least a supplement to everyday life. He also feels insistently the solicitations of the other, and he experiences an impulsion to throw himself into the flux of circumstance. The body is the prison house of the irretrievably finite soul, but it is also the temple of the earth-pledged spirit. It is so simple to conceive intellectually and so difficult to endure: a clear reflection on my life yields an irreducible ambivalence that I must always keep close to me. World rejection and life affirmation are romantic poses that hold out a nostalgic hope for reconciliation. Freud, who propounded the dualism of Eros and Ananke, is a far better guide than are Schopenhauer and Nietzsche: the individual is constitutively unreconciled to the world, a species-being with the quirk of self-enclosure.

I move back to the premodern civilizations to find aid in my effort to connect to the world erotically. The consequence of the radical separation of the self from its conventional attachments and its return to community, refreshed by contact with transcendence, is a form of disposing oneself toward existence in which one is simultaneously alongside and above life. Think of the wisdom of Jesus, that one gains oneself by losing oneself and that one should be in the world but not of it. Reflect upon the Hindu doctrine of nonfruitive action in the *Gita*, that one should devote oneself wholeheartedly to one's tasks but should refrain from hoping for their success or fearing their failure. Remember Socrates, who bore his existence so lightly and yet so seriously, full of fleshly joy but ready to die rather than exile himself from Athens. Meditate on Hasegawa's thought that the perfection of life is to compose haiku in the throes of one's death agony. And finally, dwell on Muhammad's declaration-deed that he is time. All these people were sustained by transcendence, but I must wonder whether it might be possible to be alongside and above existence without any support but one's tenacity and love for what is lovely or what might be made so in one's finite environment. If the civil savage cannot help but be ambivalent, might he not be able to craft his ambivalence into an attitude toward the erotic side of life that honors the truth about the totality of existence? The civil savage is attracted by the depth and intensity of paradox in the lives that exemplify the premodern civilizations. Postcivilized modernity has lost this fine paradox that affirms the world fully and yet with reservation and is a way of being true to life and love.

I cannot resort to transcendence, so if I am to be above life while I participate in it, I must bend back upon myself and discover within myself an independent purchase on being. Descartes gained such a hold in the rational idea of perfection, Kant in practical reason, and Schopenhauer, who demystified reason, in the imagination. In each of these cases, transcendence still cast its shadow through the objectivity of the idea or image, which was held apart from the self and, therefore, became regulative over it. My whole effort is to avoid this modern delusion of a greenhouse mind, a beautiful schizophrenia, which is really a prescription for killing time, for practicing dying. I want to find my way into the world of pleasure, not to hold myself back from engagement, yet I seek to preserve my judgment over the world as a whole, never to lose my human-all-too-human dismay at the vale of tears. These are the requirements for sanity and for the only wholeness that can be achieved by a fractured being, ordering his conflicts without harmonizing or healing them. I must be integrally disposed toward creating and appreciating goodness through making a qualified affirmation of the world. The war for pleasure is, indeed, a battle, a twisting struggle within the self, but perhaps not without humor. What is it about my will to delight that always draws it back to contemplation of the defensive life? Am I still caught in the toils of resentment and rebellion against the world and still a selfish child? Am I simply incapable of acceding to pleasure?

All of these reflections suddenly appear to be somehow ironical. The master irony of the self-consciously erotic life is that it leads me back to its positive and valued opposite, the struggle against evil. Is pleasure all the more rich and intense when it is experienced against the background of irremediable frustration? I am not speaking here of a playful and distancing irony that deprives the other-than-self of its importance, or of a pitying irony that strips the other of its autonomous magnificence. I speak of a sense of life that marvels and wonders at the other just because the other is so independent and, thus, not sufficient or necessary to the self, in fact, perhaps, the other is somewhat adverse to the self in view of the other's own precious-flawed integrity. This is the other to which and to whom I am devoted in my erotic life: like myself in its special assertion of being and in the incompletion and the failure of its dynamic. The civil savage is an ironist, using the critical categories of civilization—imperfection and frustration—to ground devotion. Just as ruthless compassion guided the defensive side of life, ironical devotion directs life's erotic dimension. I affirm a complete devotion to the pleasures of the world and an uncompromising irony toward that devotion, a serious irony that yields its own reflective pleasure, the pleasure of the unresolved and unreconciled finitude of deconstructed civilization relieved of any nostalgia. I invite you to feel this disposition, which suffuses all the rest of my meditation.

The embrace of finite life as the beginning and ending of comprehensive reflection on existence leads to a keen appreciation of the limits of all human effort to wrest from the relation of self and world any satisfactory fulfillment. A disposition to treat the goods that the world offers to the self with ironical devotion means that the decision to build bridges to fragmentary and incomplete beings must be executed by maintaining a fine balance between deliverance and indifference. A complete deliverance to finite goods involves both a loss of the self's independence of judgment, of its separation from the other, and, even more importantly, a drive to exaggerate the other's power to save existence from its pervasive failures, whereas indifference to the pleasures of the world cuts the nerve of dedication, preserving autonomy but depriving it of any scope or direction. The life-strategy of erotic hedonism exists between the volatilization of circumstance into pure imagined possibility and the fusion of imagination into concretely situational sense and feeling.

As I proceed more deeply into my free meditation, I begin to grasp the complexity of the erotic dimension of life, that an erotic attitude toward existence truly is one of rich love. There is an agony of mature pleasure, relieved of innocence yet unspoiled by disillusionment. Once I have grasped, on the defensive side of life, the irreducible scission of judgment from perception, I cannot surrender my awareness of that split when spontaneous process and deliberate activity have brought me to the point at which I am capable of cherishing and enjoying. An immature, strictly insane enjoyment is one in which I lose myself in fascination with the other and, thus, temporarily surrender my judgment so that I remain careless about what has come before and what is yet to occur. A bitter resignation to frustration keeps me distant from the other and unreceptive to its solicitations. It is simple enough to realize that one who is so resigned cannot love erotically, but it is also true that abandonment to the other is a privation of love. Cherishing includes, besides the impulse toward fusion, an element of honoring rooted in judgment. Much as I would wish to submit myself to the other, I must preserve its dignity and its separation from me, and I do so by cultivating my own difference, the irreducible isolation of my initiative. The war for pleasure is most profoundly the struggle to preserve the other as lovely and loveable in its own right, a sweet agony pervaded by the irony that the final moment is never nearness but is distance. I am permitted to enjoy the other over and over again only because I make sure to let the other be other, to retain its own imperfect integrity, and, so, the other is not made for me, and yet is capable of providing delightful surprises.

The desire for pleasure runs against the ironical sense of limitation, the acknowledgment that self and other both are equivocal, that they are worthy of being cherished and that they are failures. Every human impulse, once it has been felt, is capable of being crafted by the imagination into a generator of ideals and fantasies. The romantic movement in modern thought, particularly German idealist philosophy, seized upon this basic fact of experience and made idealization the key to unlock the nature of being. By the late nineteenth century, the ideal had been demystified, that is, deprived of any grounding in reason, and had been interpreted as a derivation or a sublimation of more primal drives of the psyche. More than anyone else, Nietzsche undertook the work of deconstructing idealism and revealed that life had its own native ideal of satisfaction that comprehended all particular desires for pleasurable objects, not as an abstraction or generalization of them, but as their vitally dynamic context: the will to be in a perpetual state of ascension and to make of its own movement the measure of its satisfaction. To be filled with vitality and to welcome the world as a source of goods to be assimilated for the enrichment and fortification of life is the standard against which the erotic side of life measures its success. As Unamuno put it, my erotic desire is "to be myself and everything else," which means the strength to connect pleasurably with all that is other to myself. This is the impossible ideal of unillusioned existence, which I appropriate not as my destiny (a constitutive ideal) or my conscience (a regulative ideal) but as a critical ideal that alerts me to my limitations and to those of the other and that vetoes the claim of specific desire to outrun its appropriate bounds.

Now I am able to focus on a feeling that has grown in me as I have opened myself more and more to the goods in the world. Ironical devotion is a form of living-into the world, an attitude or disposition of active appreciation, but it is not indifferent to emotional content. Each special pleasure is attended by particular sensations, feelings, movements, and interpretations that define it as a discriminable experience. Yet when I enjoy a pleasure in the spirit of ironical devotion, a further quality penetrates it, enhancing and muting it simultaneously. This feeling, elusive but not fleeting, might almost be called pity, but it is not that because it does not place self superior to object. It seems to be a kind of sadness, but that is not so either, because its final note is not resignation; and sadness, if it is pure rather than bitter, rebellious, or resentful, is peacefully resigned. What is a pity that fully accepts inadequacy, one's own and the other's, and that then affirms that inadequacy as desirable because it is real and must be so? What is a sadness that negates itself because it is also so sweet and affirmative, that does not efface enjoyment in any of its details but somehow heightens it? This emotion, though reflective, does not detract from resolve but strengthens it, impelling me to encounter the beloved object or other again and again, allowing me to overcome the weariness that accompanies imperfect and failed connections.

I am tempted to call my feeling the emotion of sanity, and as I dwell within it I realize that finally I have purged myself of the last vestiges of idealism, that I do love the pleasures of the world in themselves as they present themselves to me. Perhaps I should better call it the healing emotion, which refines irony of all of its negativity so that it becomes the perfect vehicle for fusing the sense of imperfection with full-blooded devotion. This is not a joy in frustration or even an acceptance of it, because the ideal of perpetually ascending life remains in awareness, as a purely functional reminder of the truth of being: it is a welcoming embrace of reality beyond clauses such as "in spite of," "because of," or "regardless of" inevitable failure. I cherish the other comprehensively for its full being, yet also selectively for the good that it offers, which seems to involve me in a contradiction. Yet the healing emotion is not contradictory, even if I can only analyze it in terms of opposites originating from the duality of perception and judgment, which is specified in this case as comprehensive acceptance and uncompromising selectivity. Suddenly I am reminded of the God of Jerusalem, particularly as God appears in the *Koran*, merciful and just. The sane and healing emotion is the proper way to affirm that "I am the creative truth," so long as I remember that (unlike the unlimited God) I must also be merciful and just toward myself.

The ideal of ascending life shifts concern with pleasure from the circumstances environing the self to the fitness of the whole person to enjoy what the world has to offer. Self-enjoyment and delight in the inwardly felt process of life as it gains in integrity, intensity, and strength is itself a primary joy, indeed, it may be called the pleasure of pleasures, which guarantees enjoyment of the goods delivered by the other-than-self and is the immediate result of delighting in them. Ascending life is the fully desublimated concrete universal, reaching out to embrace everything positive and gaining satisfaction from it. There is an inherent generosity to the Nietzschian ideal because it fuses the generalized capacity of the unified organism with alertness and receptivity to the multitude of particular goods. A narrow and selfish hedonism, which is the prevalent ethic of postcivilized modernity, seeks to bend the world to satisfy specific desires that the self has inherited from the past, and depends most deeply on a desperate will to have and to experience what the self believes it needs to complete its life. Erotic hedonism, in contrast, acknowledges the multivalence of body and psyche, the manifold connections that they can make with the other, and, therefore, contains an element of the indifference of Hindu civilization: there is no pleasure that the self needs for its own fulfillment except for the feeling of ascending life, and all of the pleasures of the world are suitable to be cherished and cultivated.

The generosity toward the world attending the disposition of ironical devotion relieves hedonism of its often insistent character, allowing Plato's strictures against the life of seeking pleasure to be muted. The great discovery of modernity for the conduct of life is that the consummation of experience appears in the sense of its dynamic rather than in the act of transcending to a greater being. The liberation achieved by making intimately concrete life its own object requires the self to affirm its irremediable incompleteness, that is, never to expect or even to hope for any permanent union with the other or for a condition of self-sufficiency. There must be joy in process rather than product, and, if one can succeed in performing this reorientation or transvaluation, one will be able to overcome, at least temporarily, the old Adam of the *Koran* who is "fretful when evil befalleth him and when good befalleth him grudging." There is no impulse to be grudging when one feels a spontaneous gratitude for the pleasures occasioned by the world. Life on its defensive side is marked by the agony of experiencing oneself as an impractical being who is destined to practicality, but the erotic dimension of life is guided by the office of loving the good for itself and for one's implication in it: in moments of ascending life one dwells in the Garden of Eden.

The discovery of the sense of life's dynamism culminates in the thought of John Dewey, who, more than any other modern philosopher, was keenly aware of the nature, condition, and structure of pleasure. I am reflecting here not on the Dewey who expounded a generalized logic of inquiry, but on the one who appreciated good so intensely and clearly that he was moved to write that great work on the art of life and life as art, *Art As Experience*. Nietzsche is the pioneering spirit who lays claim to the realm of genuine pleasure, and then Dewey follows him as the surveyor of the domain. Dewey defines the inner structure of ascending life as a series of acts, each one moving through an instrumental phase, in which disparate impulses and contents are unified in connection with aspects of the environment, toward a consummation, a transitory union of the complete individual with the other. The key insight here is into the wavelike rhythm of pleasurable experience, which is a continual process of gathering, reconstructing, and enjoying, renewed as long as there are no external intrusions and internal failures. Ascending life is not merely a formless feeling of vitality, but is a structured dynamic that approaches its perfection when each act is a consummation for itself and an instrument to the next fulfillment. In contrast, declining life is a breach in the healthy rhythm, either from frustrated and, therefore, dispersed activity, or from arrest at a point of consummation, which is motivated by fear of loss. Under Dewey's astute inward gaze the erotic side of life is revealed as an inherently ordered variety, not as the monotony that those see who believe that evil is necessary for the appreciation of good. The erotic life is fragile, but autonomous.

From the perspective of ascending life, the world is illuminated as a field of opportunity for pleasurable connection. The erotically charged self does not feel needy or even self-consciously desirous but is filled with an eagerness to participate in its circumstances through creation and appreciation. When the body is healthy, the psyche sane, and the intellect discerning, goods and the connections to them are manifold and appear as assimilable to the growing integrity of life's dynamic. The liberation into ascending life, which depends most of all on cultivation of the healing emotion, is not perplexed by the multivalence of the individual, by the inward differences of the body, by the variety of impulses and desires, or by the multitude of interpretations through which organic strain and receptivity, and emotional interest, can be connected imaginatively to the other-than-self. At a high ''vital altitude,'' to use Ortega's term, anything good will do for life. Such a generously grateful disposition, eager to enjoy and to celebrate and careful of the other's integrity, is at the opposite pole of the axis leading from the purgative zero point. Everything is possible and nothing is necessary for a purely ascending life, but that judgment does not signal irritable stagnation, suspension, and stalemate; instead it promotes an alertness to the solicitations and appeals of the other and a willingness to respond to them wholeheartedly and devotedly. At the zero point one dwells with the tensions and strains of the corporal self, whereas at life's zenith, the world is one's domain.

Let us halt for a moment at the summit of vital fullness, which is not as rare in ordinary life as it might seem to be. Most of us have experienced a good day in which we have met with fortuitous occasions and have been able to turn them to the advantage of our general plans and purposes. There are good stretches of life that may last as long as several years, when the phases of declining life are counterpoints to the ascending melody, the obscurities of the chiaroscuro. Surely, except for the victim and the curse of postcivilized modernity, the anhedonic, there are good hours and moments, consummations of small deeds and pleasant surprises, the world's gifts. A theory of pleasure should praise its object by reminders of its presence and descriptions of its structure, not only so that the object shall be known but so that it will be pursued, and, finally, self-consciously enjoyed and known in its pursuit. Vital fullness is another step along the civil savage's path to world affirmation and away from the dream of civilization. Indeed, it is the step by which he places himself on the mountaintop to survey his prospects in their most favorable aspects. From here the road leads back into the valley, into engagement with other selves and things, directed by meditation on the kinds of pleasures that arise in existence and how to distinguish the better from the worse, the moment of selectivity that tempers generosity; but stop here for a while and remember your highest vital altitude.

⬦

Erotic hedonism is an interpretation of a life that has acknowledged that the individual is destined to participation in the world of finite things, persons, and events, and that has concluded from its recognition that this world should be embraced and affirmed for the goods that appear within it to an unillusioned consciousness, purged of bitterness and resentment. The occasion for thinking out such a doctrine is the judgment that the desirability of pleasure is not self-evident or even easy to achieve in contemporary society, although it might appear at first sight that social existence today is bent on the search for mundane gratifications.

Why should it be necessary to defend and to vindicate pleasure? Such a project seems to be an invitation to selfishness, just what is least necessary and most pernicious for public discourse in light of the growing tendency for individuals to become preoccupied with their private satisfactions. Yet concern with gratification need not result in wholehearted and concrete enjoyment, but may instead indicate a desperate effort to possess objects and experiences that justify life to the self, that prove to the self that it is worthy to exist. At least in the United States, pleasure is not, I believe, valued for itself, but is often a symbol for the self that it has achieved a state of secular grace. Protestantism still exerts a grip over life, obscuring actual occurrences by transvaluing them as signs of the soul's condition, only now that condition is measured not in terms of fitness for salvation but according to shifting standards of worldly success.

The quest for self-justification through collecting achievements and things is a form of what Martin Heidegger called humanism, the understanding of existence through its relation to preconceived individual and social interests. Such striving is the most abstract of the humanisms because it refers to self-feeling and not to any particular connections to the other. The search for the grace of success is indifferent to the content of its consummations, taking its enjoyment from the reflection on having had something occur that is deemed worthwhile or having appropriated some object that is supposed, usually according to a social criterion, to be possessed. Heidegger thought that humanism should be displaced in favor of the "dignity of being": that is, we should disembarrass ourselves of our practical prepossessions and become receptive to that which sustains and enfolds our interests, especially our interest in the self. The civil savage follows Heidegger in his criticism of humanism, attempting to shift priority from self to world, but departing from the master in cherishing good, not being-itself.

The root distinction among pleasures made by the erotic hedonist divides the objective from the subjective, setting up an essentially moral demand on the self. Now we come to a decisive point in this free meditation, at which I base my judgments on a prescription, a preference, at which life strategy is not bound tightly to the description of life. My first ruthless act of selectivity is to command myself to refrain from indulging in subjective pleasures for their own sakes. I mean by subjective pleasures, those that gather about feelings of self-esteem and self-inflation, the satisfactions of having gained boons and acquirements that give me a sense of security and sometimes of superiority. Why should I cut myself off from the pleasures of self-enclosure, permitting them only transiently, as they arise spontaneously, and as means to prepare myself better to participate in the goods of the world, never allowing myself to plunder the world for sensations and perceptions to feed solipsistic reveries of self-congratulation? Are not the pleasures of self-enclosure just that, pleasures? Why should I not seal myself into consoling and exciting dreams, utilizing external reality to provide me with sustenance and with material for self-glorifying fantasy? I cannot answer these questions with argument but only with emotion, with reasons of the heart. I feel a terrible despair at the prospect of closing myself up, of creating a second, idealized life to compensate for the one that I live in the world. Additionally, perhaps, the appeals of self-inflating fantasy have been eroded for me by their failure.

Failure to do what? I am no longer desperate. The search for the secular grace of success is based mostly on a lack of self-confidence, on a need of the self to feel strong enough to suffer the assaults and defeats that mark its efforts to gain a foothold in the world, to survive and prosper. It is possible to gain sufficient confidence to realize that assault and defeat are inevitable, and that no frustration should be invested with absolute meaning. From such confidence can follow an ease with the world, a carefree disposition that replaces self-inflation with self-acceptance and desperation with irony. If I have no insistent drive to feel good about myself, because I feel at home with myself even when I punish myself with guilt, I can deploy my imagination not to construct or appropriate compensating and self-absorbing fantasies, but as a fluid medium to generate and appropriate scenarios for connecting with others. These scenarios can range from pure fictions, which show me the world I live in through their opposition to it, to what John Dewey called "experimental ideals," visions of highly concrete goals for my activity. In between those two poles are all of the fictions that show me possibilities for relating to others, even if I will never actualize them, but will simply delight in their being made present to me as possibilities. The imagination in its own way is objective if it is not turned to self-inflation and self-consolation.

By turning away from self-absorbing fantasy, the civil savage is a radical realist, not merely a phenomenologist who distinguishes intentionality from its object, but a lover of externality who is impassioned by otherness and by objective pleasure. The essence of objective pleasure is satisfaction in connection with the other-than-self, with that which resists complete assimilation into the self, retaining its stubborn independence even at the moments of most intimate union. With such a view I can consider erotic hedonism in a far more positive way than I have before. The subjective pleasures of self-enclosure yield consolation and security at the cost of excitement—not excitation, but the full-blooded engagement with the other, fraught with a measure of risk and surprise, of a tension demanding alertness and finely honed wit. Objective pleasure is exciting, vivid in its indetermination, demanding of volitional and emotional flexibility and the resources of cognition. It is involving through the movement toward completion and not through the contemplation of the completed, which is the consummation of subjective pleasure. The experience of objective pleasure is that of love brought to its most condensed and concrete actualization, passing beyond the distinction between selfishness and altruism, which is rooted in the phenomenon of subjective pleasure. Its pursuit is a moral discipline of honoring, indeed, of glorifying, the world.

The war for pleasure is a moral discipline, a program of training to be fit to enjoy the goods of the world sufficiently to love the conditions necessary for their appearance. In making the claim that I seek to love the aspects of otherness that produce pleasure and not only the pleasures themselves, I cross a boundary that I have drawn throughout my preceding reflections. I sense that I am being drawn beyond the problem of conduct and toward my relation to being-itself. Can the erotic side of life be separated so sharply from its defensive aspect as I have done, or does the struggle to overcome adversity interpenetrate so intimately with enjoyment that the two of them can never be made intelligible in isolation from each other? If I dare to try to love the conditions for pleasure, do I not throw myself into an embrace of the world in all of its appearances, since I will soon learn that the factors productive of good are also bound inextricably to those which engender evil and that they often generate both?

Much as I would like to avoid the question of whether I can affirm the world, it keeps arising at every step of my journey. The great philosophers of life at the turn of the twentieth century privileged the experience of vitality in struggle, which is the mediation between defense and love. Josiah Royce's dedication to ceaseless striving, Nietzsche's project of self-overcoming, and William James's welcome of risk all betoken an insight into the necessity of pain and discomfort for the achievement of authentic pleasure. Life-strategy, for them, was the policy of self-consciously turning evil into a means to good and of picking themselves up to renew the fight when that policy failed. They were the heirs of Hegel without his consolation of a detailed theodicy: they placed the burden of the absolute on their own shoulders, even if they sought sometimes to shift it to transcendence. Then I think of the strugglers' interlocutors, such as the Mexican José Vasconcelos and the wise expatriate Santayana, who declared themselves for unalloyed pleasure and eschewed the project of theodicy. I am temperamentally at one with Santayana's liberating criticism of Puritanism, his declaration in *The Life of Reason* that pleasure need not be excused and that, indeed, it should be praised. Yet I cannot rest with Santayana because my love begins to outrun the isolated moments of gratifying connection with the other. I dwell on the potentialities of the other to forge bonds and on my own participation, my work, in making linkages, and then, more passively, on an appreciation of the dependency of erotic satisfaction on so many adverse phenomena that I would normally reject. I still do not accept the idea that I must taste evil fully to enjoy the good, but I am better disposed to the world, more generous in extending my impulse to cherish.

I stand between the Puritans and their critics, acknowledging that the former are correct in the matter of strategy and that the latter are accurate in their appreciation of the self-sufficiency of the good. If I am to engage in the world unreservedly, I must be willing to fight for pleasure and to take up as much negativity as I can into an integrity of positive connections, but if I am to honor the good I must not confuse it with evil, even with the adversity that I have absorbed into a satisfying connection. I incorporate vitality in struggle into my conduct of life as a gift of vital fullness and surplus, which permits me to place obstacles in favorable relation to advantages, and to sharpen an edge of militancy in my hedonism. I also surround my struggling joy with the passion of union, which then spreads from its moments of consummation to color the conditions for those moments. Such passion has strict limits and cannot be seduced by any intellectual recognition of the interdependence of all things. I understand now why I seek to love the conditions necessary for the appearance of goods. I do not affirm being-itself or the world as a whole, but meditate on concrete experiences of pleasure, which have the healing power of reflecting back on what engenders them, illuminating the contexts in which they arise with their goodness. This is not theodicy, which tries to justify evil; it is the civil savage's alternative to modern civilization's resolution of the problem of evil. A passionate militancy justifies nothing, but it redeems stretches of space and time in direct proportion to my fitness and capacity to enjoy.

The second distinction among pleasures made by the erotic hedonist separates the simple from the difficult. I shall not denigrate simple pleasure as I did subjective pleasure. Direct and effortless enjoyment of some aspect of the world is the source and sustainer of the erotic side of life and in its absence there can be no unillusioned love of the world. Indeed, the curse of anhedonia is to resist the solicitations of pleasurable persons and things in order to sustain a posture of bitterness, resentment, and rebellion toward existence. Simple pleasures are the marvelous gifts of life, signaling both a substantial congruence of self and circumstance, and the contingency of that congruence. Think of taking in the dawn of a new day, breathing the fresh morning air, being filled with the rhythm and melody of a song, witnessing a joyful smile, or tasting a favorite food. Delight in simple pleasures requires only that one resist any impulses to reinterpret them in terms of a wider context of grievances against life. Receptivity to direct joys is the greatest contributor to the condition of vital fullness, and habituation to them the dynamizing element of ironical devotion. Unbidden goods are primal, giving sufficient evidence that human life is not exhausted by perspective and interpretation, but that its domain runs beyond the deliberate interest of the self. The fulfillment of the quest for being is the common and homely experience of simple pleasure, the original basis of love and gratitude.

Yet easy delights are not sufficient for the civil savage. Fortified by vitality in struggle the erotic hedonist seeks to extend the reign of pleasure beyond spontaneous and habitual connections to bonds that demand the exertion of the complete person, the integrity of spirit, psyche, and flesh. The difficult pleasures are those that link self to other through endeavors requiring concentration, skill, fortitude, and observance. All of the arts that promote ascending life, such as cooking, making love, conversing, disciplined inquiry, healing, repairing and restoring, creating, and driving cars, among a multitude of others, yield difficult pleasures; that is, joys that are tinged by a vital memory of the effort needed to achieve them, since that process of self-overcoming is present, though subdued, even in moments of consummate mastery. The difficult pleasures are ever shadowed by a temptation to give up on their further pursuit, because they always partake of the need to surmount negativity. The virtue of the civil savage is to resist that temptation, because the difficult pleasures are the fullest realizations of the good and the actively personal contributions of the self to the world. Through simple pleasures I am invited to enter into the world and through difficult joys I respond to that solicitation with creative initiative. The erotic hedonist enjoys both.

The distinctions among pleasures that I am drawing here are not exhaustive, but are those that are relevant to guiding the civil savage through his career in the postcivilized world. The division between objective and subjective pleasures is made in light of the temptation, which appears in a horizon voided of transcendence, to fall back upon self-indulgent fantasy as a source of comfort, compensation, and consolation, and, perhaps, even more as a diversion from the struggles necessary to connect with stubbornly independent otherness. It is also a criticism of the tendency of utilitarianism to transform exterior reality into a means to self-enclosed individual gratification, leaving public life under the reign of functional convenience. The addition of the difficult to the simple pleasures is similarly meant to draw the self outside its circle of ease and familiarity into active constitution of being. Here again, narrow expediency is the threat to erotic fullness, beckoning toward passivity rather than towards the work required to consummate being in complex and intense relations that forge an integral union with the other.

These distinctions pass over the traditional division between higher and lower pleasures and goods, which is characteristic of the world civilizations. In the West the Platonic legacy has privileged contemplative over active fulfillments, and the Pauline tradition has granted priority to the goods of the spirit over those of the flesh. In both cases the ground of preference is the wish for a permanent satisfaction or at least for one that is relatively secure from disruption or from contingent and accidental frustration. Even in the modern period the same desire for durability has marked reflection on the good. Descartes and Kant sought to find within the confines of subjectivity a sustaining principle in the form of an idea, and Nietzsche differed from them only in placing perfection in a temporal rather than in an eternal mode. The strategy of civilization has always been to find a stable point of repair for the troubled self, which could also be affirmed as good. Knowledge, virtue, ideal beauty, faith, and grace allow the self to dwell within itself, untroubled by the vicissitudes of mutating things and alien refractory personalities: such overarching ideals appeared to be self-sufficient and, therefore, provided strength for the individual to withstand pain and failure. These are the higher pleasures because they are the seeds and the flowers of belief in a transmundane reality, which is untarnished by the incompletion of everyday life.

The civil savage does not reject the goods and satisfactions that have been privileged by the world civilizations, at least those that do not depend on a special gift of grace, and that can be achieved by initiative, but he does not prefer them to passionate and fleshly union. Indeed, he undertakes a transvaluation of the traditionally esteemed pleasures, interpreting them as means to a fuller engagement with mutating and surprising things and persons. Consider, for example, the Kantian good will in its most generous and full-blooded sense of the disposition to treat the other person as an end, never as a means only. The civil savage shares with Kant a joy in beholding the good will and its works, but he does not cling to that will as ''the only good without limitation,'' as a moral certainty to which the self may always recur for its unquestionable self-definition. Instead, for the civil savage, the good will is the attitude through which he can elicit from the other person the potentialities for erotic union: the good will is the servant of a richer love, not the essence of love. The categorical imperative here is bounded, at its inception, by receptivity and trust (it is, for example, more important to

accept another's promise than to keep one's own) and at its consummation by real connection (the delight in caring for the other through ful-
filling the promise). Thus, the rule of promise-keeping is part of a wider
act in which the end of erotic connection tempers the rigor of autonomy,
preserving the end-in-itself but not isolating it. The constitution of the
moral relation is an objective and difficult pleasure, but the joy intrinsic
to the exercise of good will is not the finality of that relation: fulfillment
is enjoyment of the total act of love in each concrete instance. The civil
savage is directed toward objective pleasures, simple and difficult, the
latter of which often include as components the traditionally higher
goods. I might say that I profane what has been sacred in order to invest
the profane with as much holiness as it can bear.

The curse of anhedonia in postcivilized modernity takes, most generally, the form of rejecting the struggle to achieve objective pleasures
and of accepting in their stead, often with a desperate enthusiasm, substitute pleasures, which have been prepared for the self by consumer
industries and the mass media of entertainment. We live in an environment of substitute pleasures, which are simple, though not refreshing
and vibrant as are the gifts of the world, and which are directed toward
self-satisfaction and complacency. The pleasure, instilled by propaganda, of feeling self-expansion through identification with national
power; the sense of superiority over the weak and inept fostered by
situation comedies; the satisfaction of success gained by possessing
"quality" merchandise; the mild sensation of drinking a light beer or
of smoking a low-tar cigarette; and the pumped-up amazement at something that has been contrived to be "cute" are but a few examples of a
multitude of experiences in which connection with the other must be
invested with an imaginary aura and enhanced with self-feeling in order
to seem to be a consummation. It is not entirely accurate to call substitute pleasures instances of "repressive desublimation," as Herbert Mar-
cuse did, although they are also that. More deeply, they are shields for
the self against the world, permitting it to feel embedded in a context
of meaning, immune to risk and linked to a pseudo reality, the *imaginaire*, the dispensation of advertising. Substitute pleasure is the externalization of Schopenhauer's pessimism, essentially a compensation for
having to suffer the frustrations of defensive life.

Objective pleasure is the culmination of the erotic hedonist's life; I
now grasp fully what it is that I have been seeking in my free meditation
and plant myself squarely in the valley or, better, on the streets. Nega-
tively, I have been fighting to liberate myself from all of those experiences that demand that I supplement them with self-generated images

and sensations in order to affirm that they are worthwhile to undergo. Positively I have been struggling to take myself outside myself, but not away from myself, in order to honor real individuals—things and persons—through enjoying the qualities that I can elicit from them through care and attention. I think back to my reflections on the defensive side of life, to the deep cut severing perception and judgment, and realize that I have now succeeded in fusing them, albeit momentarily, in the enjoyment of objective pleasure, which knows through affirming, which is not bewildered, but which finds its way open-eyed into the wilderness of the finite other, and emerges from it laden with the treasure of particularity. There is a fine balance here between the delight in passion and the joy in service, the passivity of reception and the activity of constitution, which is always threatened with disturbance. Passionate militancy and ironical devotion hold this balance against the slackness of self-enclosure and the harshness of nihilistic rebellion. To love the pleasures of the world, to bring them into being through mutuality, is the civil savage's deepest affirmation and his strategy.

Among the difficult and objective pleasures offered by the world to the erotic hedonist, sexual union is the most indicative consummation, the one demanding the most of the self and calling forth its fullest resources. My claim here is not that all of the other pleasures are somehow derived from sexual gratification, through such mechanisms as sublimation and displacement, nor that other pleasures should be subordinated in a hierarchy to the expression of sexual delight, but that the form of the good, in its most positive and complete aspect, is displayed in the sexual connection. The essence of sexual encounter is the mutual deliverance of the impassioned flesh, in which each partner seeks to realize in the other an intense and self-sufficient satisfaction; that is, I take no regard for my own pleasure, but strive to gratify the other, and in my efforts I receive satisfaction, both from what the other gives to me and from my own giving. In a fulfilled sexual experience Dewey's ideal that the instrumental phases of action should themselves be consummations is actualized, because all of the preparations for climax are distinctly gratifying, each one of them a special good that might be sought for itself. Indeed, although sexual activity builds toward a climax, it need not reach one to be worthwhile: its deepest appeal is not in the moment of release but in all of the sensations and perceptions that are the concrete issues of a cherishing disposition.

Sexual pleasure, as I am interpreting it, is the paradigm for all difficult pleasures. The erotic hedonist as sexual lover employs intellect to understand the partner's desires and fears, and to learn how to harmonize the former and dispel the latter in order to produce a welcoming attitude of active receptivity. Sexual pleasure, however, is centered in the psyche, which must be alert and ready to enjoy all of the partner's expressions of passion and through that joy to enhance them and expand them, because the secret of sexual pleasure is the love of passionate display: the law of sex, all that one really needs to know about it, is, as the *Kama Sutra* relates, that "passion begets passion." One must be genuinely sensible to the delights of the other in oneself in order to feel acutely the joy of gratifying. Sex, then, is also the paradigm for objective pleasures because its object is another enfleshed self, in full dimensionality and capacity to respond and to surprise, whose autonomy must be honored and fortified, whose character and emotions must be appreciated sympathetically, and whose body must be prized and nurtured, even at the moments of deepest passion. For the civil savage there is no more integral contact with a person than sexual pleasure.

My account of sexual pleasure is not, I am aware, the most familiar one. Indeed, in a society permeated with anhedonia and anxiety, the compelling core of sex tends to be drawn upon, without ever being grasped, to procure simple and substitute pleasures. Sex as a simple pleasure has come to mean a selfish pursuit of the release of tension, detached from the intellectual and emotional appreciation of another person, and, therefore, purely subjective, a contextless set of sensations, an abstraction that probably occurs very rarely, if at all, in a pure form, unalloyed with feelings of self-expansion and lust for domination. A far more significant deprivation of sex is to channel it into a substitute pleasure by diverting it from its self-created or intrinsic context into an imaginary one. Concrete sexual activity can be used as a means to enriching fantasy, resulting, finally, in the projection of the characteristics of fantasy figures on the real partner. Yet more important and devastating, sex can be understood and craved as a token of one's acceptability as a self, too often as its only measure. This temptation is so great because a fully matured sexual passion is a generous welcome of the other's being. Those who fear rejection more than they love pleasure become the victims of anhedonic society, readily exploited by predators who use the affirmation of self that clings to sex to extort money, exert domination, obtain security and protection, and satisfy their whims and perversions. Nothing undermines the erotic side of life more than to subordinate it to the life of defense, to degrade objective pleasure to a means to fortify the standing of the self in the world or to inflate its opinion of itself.

Sex, as an objective and difficult pleasure, is inextricably bound to intimacy, to the state of mutuality in which individuals relax with one another sufficiently to reveal a broad range of their judgments of and responses to the world, especially their moods. In a genuine intimacy each partner maintains a fine inward balance between honoring the other's expressions and evaluating them according to an idea of the other's persisting character and essential good, the "better self." Both balance the wish and, indeed, the obligation to disclose the range of their emotions and judgments freely against an evaluation of what would help and hinder the other to thrive. Intimacy is obviously destroyed by the technical manipulation of emotions and understandings, but it is also dissolved by the myth of complete sharing, which is often a way of depriving a partner of independence by forcing him or her to submit to judgment, or of exploiting a partner by abusing with brutal frankness. The disposition of ironical devotion reaches its fruition in intimate relations, where concern for the other places a check, even if minimal and marginal, on disclosure, and a germ of distrust pricks the self lightly, reminding that the other is also failed and frustrated flesh. Intimacy is the seedbed in which sex grows, in which the risk of displaying and enjoying passion can take firm root and be renewed with least anxiety. It is also a good, a pleasure, in its own right and can be enjoyed as a dimension of a friendship that is not expressed sexually.

One of the profound corruptions of postcivilized modern life is the promiscuity of self-disclosure. Loneliness, isolation, and insecurity have become so pervasive that many people resort to ad hoc and pseudo intimacies in order to communicate their joys and sorrows, vent their enthusiasms and resentments, and, most importantly, relieve their feelings of inadequacy. The substitute pleasure of therapeutic relations, in which a circle dance of doctor-patient or confessor-penitent replaces mutual appreciation and support, threatens to banish from social life the notion of intimacy as a good. Therapeutic revelation does not ask for attentive intelligence, emotional sensitivity, and physical cherishing, but only for acceptance as "recognizably human" and perhaps some advice and a stroke. The desperation that is so evident in such encounters, the disappointment that gnaws at them, and their vulnerability to exploitation drives others to shut themselves within themselves, closing off the channels of communication through silence or filling them with masquerades. Pandisclosure and nondisclosure, brutal frankness and technical manipulation, are the origins of selfishly abstracted sex and sex diverted to self-acceptance. The pleasure of sex and the state of intimacy out of which it grows break out of self-feeling toward engagement with the other person's particularity, giving and receiving concrete and ever-fresh sensations and feelings of gratifying connection, providing the participants with proof that the world is worthy of affirmation.

I have chosen sexual intimacy to be the paradigm for the civil savage's good, the model against which all of the other objective pleasures should be measured. The sexual encounter is so special because it unites, in their diversity and with the most intense and varied feelings, the most complete of the finite realities, personal existents, who are aware of their independence and who seek connection to that which is other than themselves. The other is, from the viewpoint of a reflection on the good, preeminently another conscious individual, possessed of an autonomous will and a necessity of judging the world according to its own interests, an end-in-itself. By directing my meditation toward the other person, I imply that the erotic life does not make a sharp distinction between the realms of persons and things. Indeed, the pleasure seeker must be disposed toward things in as similar a manner as possible as he is toward a sexual partner. I do not mean here that things are to be endowed with personality, as in the case of animism, but that they should be searched for their objectivity, for their distinctive qualities, and that they should be honored and cherished for those qualities when these are productive of satisfying connection. Even if a thing must be consumed in order to be enjoyed, or exhausted or even destroyed in its use as an instrument, it may still be treated with respect, if not with the love or devotion that is appropriately reserved for another self.

I think, for example, of the pleasure of driving, in which the car may be experienced as a second body, with its own distinctive ways of responding to initiatives and its specific capacities and limitations. Respect for a car involves becoming familiar with its operation, getting its feel under different road conditions, and, most importantly, becoming adjusted to the sensibility that it offers through its weight, shape, mode of acceleration and braking, and handling. Such familiarity results in something similar to devotion, that is, in a will to actualize the capacities of the car and to drive it within its limitations, to exploit, for example, its efficient turning radius and to refrain from pushing it beyond its proper speed. Each car offers a different potential for pleasurable driving, and achieving that particular good demands that the driver submit to the car rather than to project an imagined good upon it. The same holds true for the use of any tool and, beyond that, for the enjoyment of any object, animate or not. I acknowledge a great difference in treatment, which is based on the wonder of a stubbornly absolute and separate world of willed experience, when connection is with another person, but I do not want to carry that distinction so far that I pass over the rest of being, losing sight of its specificity and its capacity to call out devotion.

The civil savage is a lover whenever his life achieves a fullness and a surplus that permits him to delight in the world rather than merely to mobilize parts of it in order to maintain and expand his security. The defensive life inverts the erotic order, privileging the relation to the world in which the other is stripped of an independent claim to be respected and honored, and is, instead, approached as a means to be exploited or an obstacle to be overcome or eliminated. Here a deprived mode of being, that of the means-to-an-end, becomes the paradigm for connection to all realities, including persons; that is, the person is intended as a difficult or challenging thing rather than the thing being experienced as a severely limited quasi person. Mass technological society tends to efface the erotic side of life so much that nothing can be appreciated for its strength-in-weakness and its weakness-in-strength. Its substitute for erotic joy is the self-expansive satisfaction of the connoisseur who is trained to distinguish the ''finer things'' and who is disappointed with anything less, or, more commonly, of the consumer who is gratified by possessing what one is supposed to have to prove to oneself that life is worth living or that one has not been left behind others. The civil savage's love is democratic and beyond the reflective pleasures of self-esteem. Each object is cherished by him for the good that it holds potentially within the context of its finitude or of its weakness. Here, then, is the uttermost truth of the civil savage, his victory in the war for pleasure: to love the pleasures of the world is to be devoted to the real other, the finite other, which or who never appears in the guise of an ideal of perfection and which or who always has the marks of the perishable.

Can it be that it is more delightful to love the imperfect than the ideally perfect, the perishable than the lasting? Can it be that the deepest devotion is to bring the weak to a little more strength, to make the shorter last a bit longer? I do not deny that there are better and worse connections and that, therefore, the other is more or less excellent according to the criteria of the various goods. Nor do I deny that there should be a continuous stress and strain toward the better and that ideals are essential not only as measuring rods but as reminders of the reality of incompletion. Yet such concerns have all become counterpoint to the theme of enjoying the world for what it offers to me here and now, in these particular circumstances, on its own terms. If the goods of finite life are so diverse as to be incommensurable and if I have the ability to enjoy a multitude of them in many different grades, my primal disposition must be gratitude for their existence, a welcome to them as they are in themselves and in the possibilities for their own perfection. Although I will judge them sometimes against my best and most uncompromising imagination, I will not use ideal and fantasy to deprecate them but, instead, to appreciate them more acutely in their singularity. The other as genuinely other is incommensurable and unique, and finitude is bound up with uniqueness. Yes, it is more delightful to love the imperfect than the perfect, because only the real other can elicit both my respect and my care, the pleasure of receiving and of giving, each moment of the dialectic of love united to the other through ironical devotion or militant passion.

The war for pleasure is over and its plunder is sanity. The sanity of civilized life is to see through the relativity of communal conventions to a greater reality and to use the form revealed to transcendence as a guide for placing oneself back into the community, secure from fanaticism and in one's independence. Postcivilized modernity must nurture a new kind of sanity, which is not based on any model or experience disclosed to a privileged subjectivity, but which is sustained and constituted by direct encounter with the world.

The challenge held out to a clarified postcivilized consciousness is to love the pleasures of the world for their own sakes, in full awareness of their limitations. Such a consciousness must resist the temptations of the great world civilizations to declare that being is good and of modern noncivilization to replace the goodness of being with the ceaseless search for subjective satisfactions, rooted in the gratification of self-expansion. Avoiding the first temptation assures that the self will maintain its stubbornly separate integrity and its freedom to judge the world anew out of its own resources; rejecting the second temptation will keep the self open to the other, in readiness to embrace its surprising gifts and to work upon them to create more complete, intense, and complex goods. Pleasure is not a property of being-itself nor is it a state of subjectivity: it is most genuinely an emergent within a connection between self and other, born of lucidity, training, devotion, and, perhaps most importantly, attentive sensibility.

Chapter 4

Postcivilization

The dream of modernity is to surpass itself, to conceive from itself through a collective parthenogenesis its own transcendence, to generate a new period of history that nullifies the category of history or that institutes a genuine history that is no longer tainted by any nostalgia for eternity. So it has become fashionable to discourse about a postmodern era, which is only to claim that the grating irritation of contemporary life can be solved by an incantation.

Postmodernity does not designate a supersession of the modern, but is a word for the latest moment of the modern process, that moment in which the modern formula is deconstructed and all that remains is the bare wish for something new, for something that will carry experience beyond its finite confines and into a satisfactory resolution in which life becomes fluid, expansive, and comfortable. Most of all, it is a moment in which the adversities of personal existence are dispelled or, at least, no longer matter to the self-conscious individual.

Think of an imaginary landscape, an impossible landscape. You are crossing a magnificent high bridge. As you look to one side you see the vision of the contemporary technological city, a cluttered maze of commerce, gleaming here and there, but streaked irremediably with dirt and waste, dense and swarming, and pocked with specialized niches that encroach upon one another and that, though separate, do not evince any determinate limits. Then you look to the other side and see a verdant expanse of virgin nature, a green forest dotted with lakes, peaceful and welcoming, a place where you can be whole in your solitude, enveloped and pure. You feel a vertigo, as though a wind were about to sweep you off the bridge and plunge you into the river far below. The landscape, which juxtaposes culture and nature, provokes dizziness because it is impossible and intolerable in its impossibility. The crawling city, with all its purposive purposelessness, its demands on frustrated initiative, is too irritating to approach, yet the forest, even in its beauty, is too sublime, too inhuman, to prompt deliverance to it. There is something disturbingly fantastic about the forest. You could never see it this way, so sharply divided from the city. Were this a real landscape you would perceive the traces of the city in the forest; culture would already have spilled over into nature (contaminating it?). You must turn back and return to the point at which you began your trek, to ground zero of the postmodern modern, the business district of a suburb, in which all of contemporary life fuses into a similitude of normality, in which the products of impoverished exploitation simulate luxury. There you shall take your stand if you are the civil savage who wishes to love the pleasures of the world.

I take my vision to be a key to the meaning of the discourse on postmodernity. The bridge is Nietzsche's rope over the abyss, the span to the overman. Yet it does not lead to anything new, not even to a provisional novelty that would be swallowed up in an eternal recurrence. Nature, so overwhelming, will never be home to humans: sublimity engulfs beauty. It is the *mysterium tremendum et fascinans* for the spirit void of transcendence, promising repose at first glance, but concealing within itself an overpowering force, indifferent to desire. Culture, so dense, is the home that people have made for themselves, but it has outrun their ability to comprehend it. There is no way beyond the excruciating condition of being between the two in spirit, but locked into the latter in the flesh and, far more poignantly, in the psyche. Here is the clue to the postmodern moment of modernity: the modern process has worked beyond the relation between nature and culture established by civilization. In all of the great world civilizations, including the modern, culture is interpreted as the perfecting of nature or as the proper expression of a determinate human nature. Now that relation has been transformed and nature and culture stand juxtaposed to each other starkly, the first now only an unearthly dream and the second an enigmatic destiny. The postmodern spirit is trapped uneasily between a failed yearning for a nature, which is revealed as an unholy sublime sufficiently inhuman to invite conquest but too immense to be captured, and a culture that appears as an intensive complexity without integrity, an overmastering grotesque and genuine second nature. That is, the grand polemic of nature and culture has come to an end because both of the contestants have proven to be inhuman. Culture is no longer an instrumental and expressive adaptation of person to nature; it is the person's new environment.

Thus it is possible to understand many of the new ideas that fill intellectual culture with siren songs of self-abandonment. The notions that language speaks us, that all signifiers signify other signifiers, and that reality is simulation, bespeak an engulfment of personal existence in culture. Modernity takes a fateful step beyond romance, putting an end to the pious delusion of progressivism that the war of all against all could be replaced by the collective struggle to transform primary nature into an adequate habitat for the fulfillment of need and the release of expressive emotion. Nature has been transfigured and transformed into a new environment, which is as threatening as the old one and, perhaps, far less attractive. We fast approach the time when we spring not from the earth, but from a test tube, and when we end in an intensive care unit, in a hospice, or on a dissection table. Such a view has become a platitude, and I do not speak about these things bitterly and with any nostalgia for primary nature. Had nature been fit for personal existence, it would never have been remade into the superorganic. I must simply admit into my consciousness, so that it takes it over fully, the idea that culture is no longer the badge of human superiority and dignity, but is brute circumstance, a second wilderness strewn atop the first one. In distancing myself from culture I reclaim myself more vividly and even more securely than I ever could have in a civilized order.

The civil savage dwells in postcivilized modernity, the essence of which is the radical objectification of culture to the point at which it becomes environment, circumstance, and situation, rather than the mediation it once was. Human beings have always striven to cast a net of imagination over the world, but only recently and then only in the hyperindustrialized societies of the West have they succeeded in doing so. We are privy today to talk of postmodernity because the mind has finally been externalized sufficiently for consciousness to be glutted with its own tracings, so much so that it is possible to live through a day of wakefulness and perceive only tokens of fragmented signification. Even the sky betokens meteorology, but that does not mean that it has been rendered trustworthy or homely, but only that it has been interpreted imperfectly. Similarly the body can easily be lived as the anticipation of the ailments to which it will probably be subject and the treatments that it will undergo to remediate or to complicate those ills. Primary nature has been thoroughly encrusted with culture, but, of course, it has not been brought to heel. It is not that technology is out of control or that capitalism has turned everything into commodity but that human beings have at last accomplished the task of enwrapping themselves in their own works, and the clothing fits badly.

⤇

The radical objectification of culture is the intelligible outcome of the modern process that creates, paradoxically, a deep bewilderment for those who must still fight and love. It is difficult to do what is now necessary, to turn one's back on the past decisively and to prepare determinedly to thrive within a milieu that is both final and fluid. How does one exist with a success that is not successful? One may fruitfully interpret the contemporary world as the fulfillment of the Hegelian prophecy: being has been thoroughly humanized, the personal existent is absorbed by the concrete universal and perceives only the vestiges of the human-all-too-human mind. The fateful modern dare of abandoning all fixity has ended in creating a static context that forms a clearing for any finite mutation and transformation imaginable, on the condition that it is vulnerable to being surpassed by other limited and unstable entities. Everything is designed, but each thing encroaches on the others, constituting a sloppy and messy array in constant flux, a mirror of the disordered psyche in which the parts strive to gain supremacy over the whole but fail to do so, not only because they check each other mutually, but, more fundamentally, because each one is too weak to take charge and would prefer to shift responsibility to a genuinely competent and capable power.

Yet there can be no firm direction, since dynamism and diversity have become the ruling antiprinciples. We still live in the wake of modern civilization, which, from our present vantage point, can be understood as a bravely desperate effort to compose diversity into unity and change into permanence. The rhetorical devices of current public life are still those of the nineteenth century, moving equilibrium through competition, revolutionary achievement of rational community, and democratic planning for need satisfaction. The language of totality is still being spoken, but its substance is no longer hope or the mystifying justification of exploitation: it is a stimulus to feeling comfortable and to half believing that there is a whole to which appearance can be referred. Can there even be cynics when rhetoric has become completely rhetorical and the tokens of civilization function simply as incitements to feeling? The old imagined totalities were promises of future perfections and under their guidance the world we live in was created. We now know that they did not signify the actualization of their intentional objects but were motivators for getting people out into the world to transfigure it into the image of the old Adam. We are enveloped in our own works and try as we will to discover something that we have not touched, we cannot help but sense our hands everywhere. We can at last look about us and see only ourselves. The sight is not pleasant, in part because our environment provokes an immediate judgment on our worth.

I am pushing hard, struggling to erase any of the traces of nostalgia that lurk within my sensibility. It is even too heroic to wail, as Heidegger did, about the engrossing triumph of technology. The criticism of the technological order still seems to leave something untouched by the human hand, that is, the ability to think beyond the practical impulse and thereby to institute another kind of thinking, a thinking that is a thanking in Heidegger's case. There is no awful Faustian will to will that has taken over the modern mind, leading it to contrive a horrible simulacrum of itself. The truth is far more banal, though terrifying in its own way for those who crave something better than themselves. What we live with is not technology out of control but the products of our own frailty. Hegel's philosophy of nature, far more than his reflection on history, illuminates our world through its identification of essential weakness. Nature, for Hegel, is inherently unsatisfactory to the spirit because it does not have the strength to conform to a type, either in its parts or as a whole. Natural science forms abstract summaries of things, but cannot capture them exhaustively. Have we not found that the same holds true for our second nature, our culture? It is a deceptive trick to identify nature with actual entities and culture with mental designs, forgetting that effective culture is objective: this toxic chemical spill, this rusting car, this crumpled handbill, and this applied makeup. Just as Hegel wished, culture is available as fully substantial, but it is no more integral than primary nature; indeed, it is even less so, because it is a secondary complexity added to a primary ground.

Culture is not our bridge from spirit to nature, nor is it our home within the world, nor the mark of our transcendence and the badge of our dignity, and it surely is no longer the symbol of a greater reality: it is ourselves externalized and made concrete. It can never be greater than we are, in the sense of saving us from ourselves and bringing us beyond ourselves. Yet culture can certainly also be greater than we are by engulfing us and by presenting us with demands that are too rigorous for the flesh to fulfill. Idealization, which is the germ of culture that grows under the care of sensory-motor mechanisms into objects, can impose tasks that the organisms who generate and use it are too weak to accomplish.

In this process I encounter the root of postcivilized modernity. We are no longer encompassed by God or by nature, and, more seriously, in the terms of modern civilization, we are no longer challenged by the ideal: we are confronted by the things that we have made and that we continue to make in a ceaseless endeavor to overcome them. The earth is first covered over with things and then ever more layers are added, and now we are glutted, and yet we contrive more of them, half hoping that they will lead us back to nature, half fearing that result, and knowing that it will never happen.

The civil savage declares the end of modern history, which means the exhaustion of the category of history, interpreted as the story of the human endeavor to enculturate the earth and to make a habitation that is responsive to human desire. That history was constituted by the dialectic of spirit and flesh, self and world, subject and object, and its dynamic was the overcoming of alienation by creative transformation: technical art to serve survival, political art to secure peace and initiative, and expressive art to produce delight. That struggle is over and has ended in defeat; indeed, it is perverse to continue it as the detritus of culture piles up, not only the poisons, the garbage, and the vast stretches of instant ruins, but the dead signs, the symbols emptied of hope and even of the haunting heroism of despair. The ground has shifted and there is a new battle to be fought, that of culture and flesh. This battle is not, as the old one was, a project of overcoming, but is a coming to what is already present, a dis-tension and a disentangling. The civil savage must seek to understand culture as that which is not his own. It is no more his servant and no more destined to be his servant than is nature, even though it has been created by human beings. The demystification and disenchantment of culture: this is the project of the civil savage as he moves out into the postcivilized world to fight the war for pleasure.

The civil savage is the demystifier of culture, who appears at the moment of the modern process when civilization begins to deconstruct itself on account of its own failed success. The entire movement of modern self-criticism until the end of World War II was directed toward the disenchantment of the world, under the sign of Nietzsche's death-of-God decree. Nietzsche, who was painfully aware of the loss of transcendence, became possessed of the idea that human beings might withdraw their projections of final meaning into themselves and thereby regain, or even gain for the first time, an intimate contact with the sources of their creativity. His parable of the camel, lion, and child in *Zarathustra* betokened the limit that modern humanistic optimism could reach.

The formula of humanism is the deliverance of the world to will as the field for its initiative and endeavor. For Nietzsche, the humanistic project could only be fulfilled through a therapeutics in which the camel, whose strength is to bear the burden of past judgments and interpretations, gives way to the lion's self-willed negation of signification, which then passes into the innocently spontaneous initiative of the child; that is, he prescribes the instauration of a new culture in which the individual exemplar of species being becomes coincident with himself. Here Nietzsche is at one with his more democratic and progressive forebears, contemporaries, and successors. The disenchantment of the world offers, for him, an opportunity for at least some human beings to realize their essence, even if that essence be in the fluid process of self-overcoming. What is the guarantee of the actualization of that essence but the creation of culture, of the humanized world as a springboard to a new being, the overman, who will create more culture? Indeed, with Nietzsche, individuals become their own works of supersession, closing the technical impulse, the dynamic of *homo faber*, in upon itself.

All of the other influential humanisms, such as Marx's socialism and Dewey's liberalism, are faint approximations to Nietzsche's because they fail to grasp fully the challenge of hurling culture into the void out of the sheer flux of vitality. Dewey's criticism of the quest for certainty is equivalent to the project of eliminating the shadows of God from consciousness, as is Marx's polemic against alienation, but political humanism falters as it loses its ground in being, and retreats to a contrived image of humanity for its basis, regressing to the stage of the camel. The civil savage cannot but look back upon all of these efforts to wring optimism out of demystification with a sympathetic contempt. The disenchantment of the world was taken as an opportunity for a new order, which is why it could be undertaken without any real sense of deprival. Modern self-criticism, in this light, is little different from conservative apology: the criticism can be brutal and penetrating (there are no more acutely existential portrayals of the human condition than those offered by Catholic apologists) because a compensating vision has been prepared to redeem it.

Culture for the flesh is the hidden motto of progressive humanism. If we no longer can believe that God or nature responds to our needs favorably, we can still take matters into our own hands and try to make the world over in the image of our own best hopes. The only difference between Nietzsche's defense of nobility and aristocracy, and the Marx-Dewey advocacy of community is in the definition of the hope. Nietzsche's special significance is that he went to the root of the problem by carrying through a thorough demystification: if the signifiers of transcendence are fragments of human desire projected on an imaginary field, then the self-conscious recognition of them as imaginary leaves the future open to an indefinite range of possible commitments. Nietzsche hoped to contain the explosion of possibility by relating it to an unencumbered vitality that had been tempered by assimilation of the past and of culture. He suggested that such an intimate incorporation of the judgments of the race would allow a new form of innocent being to be born. There is no more sublime apotheosis of culture than this one, a complete personalization in which the irremediably alien and unhealthy is destroyed or passed over, and the compatible and strengthening is made intimate. Nietzsche is the great assayer, assigning himself the task of preparing for the overman by taking up the burdens of the camel and then forcing the negation of the lion, but never returning to the child. Now the civil savage glances back and sees that Nietzsche did not prepare for the overman, but simply encountered within himself the dialectic of culture and flesh.

Culture and flesh. Nietzsche had already grasped the next moment of the modern process imperfectly in *The Use and Abuse of History*, and had begun the demystification of culture haltingly. He argued there that confidence in life had been gravely impaired by a withering skepticism that sprang from the accumulation and encrustation of judgments over the centuries. Modern consciousness, he warned, was refracted through layers of interpretation and had lost contact with its primary source; it was imperiled with a dissipation of vitality because it had lost any sense of the adequacy of its judgments to a spontaneous ground and, therefore, existed rootlessly and self-referentially in an environment in which signifiers referred only to other signifiers and not to a primary or given reality. In this sense he was the precursor of contemporary poststructuralism, as he was in other ways the forebear of every current of twentieth-century modernism. In his early philosophy of history, Nietzsche called for the recuperation of vitality through a decisive act of will in which the past would be transvalued as the nutritive substance of present intention, foreshadowing his dialectic of camel, lion, and child. His demystification was incomplete only because he refused to confront the irreversibility of culture's tyranny, its precipitation as a true second nature that could not be surpassed in a new beginning, but might be loosened or decoupled from within. His legacy to the civil savage is the agony of the camel and the lion, ever renewed as the acceptance of and the rebellion against the necessity of inscription by the product of human creation.

What is the civil savage but everything the child is not? Nietzsche, the exemplar of all of the humanists, took his stand on the creative will, on its capacity for transforming the world and for transfiguring inward human nature itself. The civil savage stands within the flesh, which, in the age of artificial intelligence and the externalized imagination of TV, is for him the last redoubt of reality. It is flesh that lacks nobility and resists community. It is both too much and too little to say that culture has turned against the flesh; too much because it is consubstantial with the constitutive impulse of human existence to compensate for its frailty and too little because conceiving of a war between culture and flesh disregards the extremity of enculturation, which penetrates into the depths of body and psyche. One of the consequences of demystifying culture, of objectifying it, is to acknowledge its power to form life and to be seized by the doubt that this power can even be deflected, much less directed or overcome. I become, as Nietzsche foresaw, a hypothetical or experimental being who evinces a cultural possibility. That means I can never even hope to be a child. Yet I cannot say candidly that culture has obliterated and effaced flesh; there is still a difference and that difference is grasped in my inward sense of my vital feeling, in a primary responsiveness that may or may not be conditioned; it simply seems that it cannot be overcome and is, thus, my opening to the world, my hammer claw for deconstructing culture.

Postcivilized modern life is deconstructed, that is, de-structured, in reference to the absence of any unifying principle for directing, organizing, and creating culture. Sartre's vision, in *Nausea*, of a surfeited and aimless agglomeration of stubbornly particular things, each one in the way of the others and rendering all of them superfluous, now must be sharpened and clarified to include and emphasize cultural objects. For Sartre, there was still something that differentiated culture from those kinds of being that appear to be more spontaneous, its ideality and conformity to design; that is, culture, though its mediating function was problematic, was somehow satisfying to spirit, the for-itself, by virtue of its definition, its essentiality. Poststructuralism has moved a step beyond existentialism by questioning the spirituality of culture and by pushing it into the world and surrounding consciousness with a welter of signifiers. Each cultural object refers to one or more others, but the entire complex of them has no unitary meaning, not merely in the sense of the possibility of subsuming them under a coherent idea, but, more deeply, in the sense that the cultural aggregate lacks importance and significance. It has become an array of facilities and utilities, each of which can be manipulated to provoke perceptual and emotional consequences, but those results may not always or even usually be the ones that have been prevised in their designs.

No wonder a thinker like Jean Baudrillard can write about an indefinite sequence of simulations, an endless round of anticipatory testing and monitoring, which produces a stasis of countervailing activities. Life is a servomechanism with only itself to regulate, its only movement to contrive ever more processes of self-adaptation. The flesh here is drawn into culture in order to become a component of an instrumental complex. Even Baudrillard's vision contains too great an element of nostalgic optimism. If the outcome of modernity is the creation of an all-pervading simulacrum, we have been deprived of the opportunity and, perhaps, even the impulse to overcome ourselves, but in return for this sacrifice (if that is the proper word), we have gained a sort of home with an intelligible, if not significant, structure. The truth, and there is a truth to be told here, is that there is no self-referential cultural homeostasis, no Moloch of culture consuming its worshippers. There is, instead, a bewildering fragmentation, an ex-centricity, a de-centering, and a resulting exposure of inherent frailty and weakness. Indeed, the more interventions and monitors are heaped upon one another, the more boards of inquiry, investigative committees, arbitrators, and special prosecutors are conjured forth, and the more tensions and gaps appear, the less any plausible integrity can be discerned.

The normal experience, and here I mean, in Heidegger's language, what the self encounters "proximally and for the most part" in its "average everydayness," of postcivilized modernity is paradoxical and two-sided. From one viewpoint, culture has become utterly tyrannical, engrafting itself on the flesh, permeating the psyche, and overwhelming the mind. Unamuno's "man of flesh and bone" exists no longer, having been replaced by a new entity, which the Canadian philosopher George Grant calls in reflection upon the astronaut, "half metal and half flesh." There is no basis for undertaking a Socratic quest for self-knowledge because all that such a search would reveal would be the results of a previously enacted imagination and certainly not an uncorrupted source of being.

From another perspective, as human existence becomes fused with culture, it distances itself from its own creations, which appear to it to be other than itself, not precisely alien, because that would be carrying criticism to the dialectical extreme of a full negation of a putative totality, but simply different in an eerie sense. "We are technology," as Grant proclaims, but at the same time technology is mere environment. What does it mean to watch TV, which simultaneously engulfs and constitutes sensibility, and is so easily dismissed? What does it mean to take a "mood-altering" drug and to observe its effects upon oneself in semidetachment? What does it mean to hold a belief, not because (as Nietzsche said) one "believes in belief," but because it makes the negotiation of social relations more convenient, because it is judicious, whether or not it is true? The camel and the lion coexist in an irritating embrace, draining one another of their vitality.

Max Horkheimer, in *The Eclipse of Reason*, identified with capitalism a society that is planned in all of its parts but unplanned as a whole, and hoped that it would be transcended by an order based on substantive reason, in which genuine human needs would be discriminated through discourse and then fulfilled with creative ingenuity. The civil savage knows, forty years after Horkheimer wrote his book, that it is not capitalism that deprives him of a vitally intelligible order, but the loss of civilization and the triumph of culture. Capitalism, indeed, has been and continues to be a great decivilizing engine, through cultivating an abstract measurement of success and money, which homogenizes importance and lends a pseudo-objectivity to value, but it does not by itself generate any specific complex of cultural objects. Modern culture, which is in great part energized by capitalism, is simply an expression of the ways in which a multitude of human needs, desires, and whims have sought satisfaction. It is not even possible any more to perform a constructive criticism of desires aimed at determining which ones are authentic and which are spurious and specious. Here is the historical justification for poststructuralism: desire itself has become, how much we cannot know, a response to the externalized imagination, to culture. What we encounter in our environment, our second nature, are the fates of desires, and it is frequently impossible to decipher from those destinies the impulses that initiated and for some time guided them.

Having drenched himself in contemporary cultural criticism, the civil savage is ready to return to his erotic hedonism, armed with the categories through which he must understand his war for pleasure. Postcivilized modernity leaves the individual center of conscious life with nothing of his or her own but vital feeling—responsiveness. The deepest hope that has been lost in the modern process is that one can feel serious about making demands upon the world. We live now in an environment that is saturated with the results of past demands—for example, nuclear weapons and power plants, toxic waste dumps, racist and sexist ideologies, expressionistic art, advertisements, psychotherapies, welfare systems, narcotics, and acne medications. Any of these can be altered, new objects can be created and old ones destroyed or rehabilitated, and sets of them can be coordinated into new complexes, but they cannot be unified coherently on the whole and they cannot be referred back to a primary nature. So it comes time to treat culture as a wilderness replete with perils and pleasures, to take a step beyond Ortega's "dehumanization of art" to the dehumanization of culture as a whole and to acknowledge the exteriorization of culture with its separation from will and its return to the self as pleasure and pain, as that which provokes response. At least for the moment nothing can substitute for feeling. Self-mastery means mood management, the fitness to enjoy.

My analysis of postcivilized modernity culminates in the insight that the world is not the proper home for human beings and that all efforts to make it one through the creation of culture only exacerbate estrangement. My reflections do not erupt in a historical void but are the intelligible continuations of the modern discourse, which first liberates consciousness from any attachment to a transmundane reality and now must confront the consequences of freedom, the exteriorization, fragmentation, and dynamization of culture. Postcivilization means the loss of the dream that compensated for the death of God, the fantasy that once human beings were unlinked from the limitations of an imagined transcendence they would seize the opportunity to remake their circumstances so that their environment would become satisfactory to them.

The death-of-God decree is succeeded by the acknowledgment that culture has become dehumanized at the same time that it remains all too human. We can produce more determinate effects than we have ever been able to generate before, although these results may not always be the ones that were precisely intended, but we cannot create a coherent world. Everything bears some meaning, refers to something else, but nothing organizes the rest of things into a significant pattern: everything is possible and nothing is necessary, not even the project of making a home of the world, which now merely functions as a bit of nostalgia that sets up a screen between self and circumstance, the better to promote a fragile comfort and a justification for going to work.

The civil savage announces that all of the exits from modernity have been sealed, and that postmodernity is the stark wish of modern consciousness not to be itself. It is a hope evacuated of all content, and the pure proclamation of the form of novelty projected into an indefinite future. In what direction could an exit lead? Nature has been thoroughly demystified intellectually and now it is being practically stripped of any romance by biotechnology. The products of high culture have been traced to their social and psychological determinants and have been absorbed into propaganda, advertising, and entertainment. A cultural revolution is a deceptive illusion because there is no image of genuine desire to ground it. Postcivilized modernity is the partial victory of every human desire, the triumph of what the critic Irving Babbitt called "expansive emotion" under the sign of "efficient megalomania." Yet expansive emotion cannot be the basis for creating a world because it is a name for the aggregate of desires, each one encroaching upon the others through systems of collective organization. No desire achieves a clear fulfillment in modern life, but each one finds an equivocal expression: the world appears as an array of smudged codes. According to Kierkegaard, "purity of heart is to will one thing." It is just such decisiveness that has become impossible, because there is no integral context to which to refer such a will.

The deeply irritating point of contemporary life is the relation of self to culture, which must appear to me simultaneously as mine and not-mine, as the very basis of my possibility for surviving and as an alien collection of dynamisms that invade me and threaten to overwhelm me. Following Nietzsche's imagery of nutrition, culture gives me a case of indigestion. I am in the condition of the person who must eat tainted food because there is no other food available, but who knows that it will cause extreme discomfort later, even as it helps to sustain life. Following Sartre's suggestion of an existential psychoanalysis, which reveals the feeling of one's relation to being, I taste a filmy rot corrupting the objects around me and yet I must incorporate them into my own dynamism practically and appreciatively. I must poison myself in order to live, as must everyone around me. The world has become abusive as a general rule: my totem animal is the garbage fish of the Great Lakes, which has genetically adapted to a polluted ecological niche. Or perhaps I shall learn to worship the South American cockroach or the Norway rat, or the stray dog or homeless cat. All of these contemporary forms of life have made successful adaptations to an unsuccessful second nature and perhaps they can teach me, just as the forest animals taught the early practitioners of yoga the secret of how to live today. The vitally successful species in postcivilized modernity win through the formula of strength within weakness, through a complete embrace of environmental failure, indeed, a devotion to it to such an extent that they would die without it.

Unamuno noted in *The Tragic Sense of Life* that one must poison oneself in order to live well. That is a basic law of life that can only be affirmed unequivocally once nature and culture have been demystified. Postcivilized modernity is a privilege, not because it provides an opportunity to ascend to a new level of life and to participate in the creation of a new age, but because it discloses what the human condition has always been and, I presume, will always be. Human existence is constituted by the substantial duality of adversity and beneficence, pain and pleasure. There is nothing more fundamental that I can imagine to say about it and, from there, if I wish to perpetuate myself, I must reflect strategically and tactically about how to tolerate and deflect adversity and how to take advantage of beneficence, so as to allow pleasure to compensate for pain. In order to live well in postcivilized modernity, I must decide to live in the truth of life, to accept that I know myself only through my responses, and to orient myself to making responses to what the world truly offers and not to an imaginary environment that I have fabricated to standardize my emotions. Now I have returned once again to the center of my reflection, in full acknowledgment and embrace of it, knowing at last that this meditation has a center: ironical devotion. Seize your vital feeling from within and then direct it to respond to the second nature that surrounds you and you may experience the distension of irony, the appetite for the equivocal.

Let me reach back to the treasure trove of the civilized past and extract from it a political temperament that will guide me through the rest of my meditation, which will be a mapping of the present culture, a tourist guide and survival manual. Throughout the modern period there has been a counterpoint to idealism, a realism that accepted and even reveled in refractory limitation. The essence of that realist spirit was captured by the nineteenth-century political essayist Walter Bagehot in his phrase ''animated moderation.'' It is possible to hold fast to all of the insights of poststructuralism, to be acutely aware of all of the losses that attend the eclipse of civilization, and still to be civil. Civility is the public expression of sanity that blends vivid emotion, a taste for worldliness, and a keen judgment of finite possibility in which perception challenges judgment and judgment steadies perception. I freely admit that Bagehot formulated his oxymoron to describe the virtue of parliamentary democracy, and that the institution he defended has become a functional mechanism to cope with the tensions created by the failures of administration, but the civil savage is a plunderer of the past and a decoupler. The political dimension of the lover is liberal, especially when the culture has become thoroughly illiberal, plagued by enthusiasm covering anhedonia and by anhedonia stifling vivacity. Far from being an anachronism, Bagehot's liberal virtue is the source of the strength that is appropriate to circumambient weakness.

The environment of postcivilized modernity is constituted by the externalization of the human mind, undisciplined by any unitary principle of organization to provide it with coherence and with any sense of easy passage for the self from one of its regions to the others. In a sense, it approximates the "pluralistic universe" described by William James in which all components are related to some others, but none is linked to all of the others. For James, the pluralistic universe was a ground for optimism, holding opportunity for novel creation and the discovery of surprising and, perhaps, beneficent entities, if only one were bold enough to take the risk. His "radical empiricism" defined an open-ended flow of lived experience, a possibly fruitful flux amenable to shaping and reshaping, a medium for art best utilized by a "happy anarchist" freed from the constraints of received forms. The pluralism of postcivilized modernity, in contrast, is one of irremediable disstructure, of the finality of incompletion, failure, and frailty; of the inevitable penetration of a fragmented and mutating culture into the flesh, as though the body were a mosaic engrafted with shards, some of them failing to take and being replaced by others, a perpetual piercing and lacerating.

The vitalistic optimism of Nietzsche, Bergson, James, and even the saner and more critical Simmel pitted culture against a life process, not against a partially determinate flesh, allowing for the hope that culture might be transcended perpetually. Culture, for them, was an expression of some of the manifold possibilities of imaginative experience, the result of the demiurge, creative will, which renewed itself spontaneously, although it betrayed a tendency to entrap itself temporarily in its creations. Anything might crop up in the process of creative evolution, which often was thought to have a generally upward tendency, a nisus

toward comprehensive, uncoerced, and complex order. Radical empiricism, the dogma of indetermination and the romance of nonfoundation-
alism, has today become a way for postmodernists to evade the limits
that hedge them from without and within. Why not think in terms of
the supersession of the dualities of spirit and flesh, of the transcendence
of alienation toward solidary community, if the terms of duality are but
the elements of perspectives generated by a mysterious process, be it a
purified Nietzschian "will to power," a Marxian "praxis," or a dynamic naturalism borrowed from the pragmatists?

Yet we are flesh surrounded and pervaded by its products, not a flow
of experience. We are determinate organisms with a measure of indetermination that indicates our incapacity to reconcile ourselves to ourselves and to one another. We ceaselessly attempt to complete ourselves
by contriving, out of our indetermination, that second world of culture,
which at last confronts us as the image of our primary division.

Radical empiricism is the dogma of the open life with a conceivably
revolutionary future, the cherished myth of the intellectual advocates of
the weak, of the radical feminists, third-worlders, anarcho-Marxists, and
Christian liberationists. Having been excluded from the advantages of
individualism, they attempt to reduce the radical separation of the incarnated spirit from unity with its environment to supposedly transient
structures of exploitation such as patriarchy, empire, capitalism, and
rationalism. Once they have performed this reduction, which involves a
flight outward from self-knowledge to a social criticism based on grievance against exclusion, an interpretation of the self in terms of how it
has been treated by others rather than how it engages the world from
within its conscious center of response, they proclaim the advent of a
community freed from the curse of individuals who take themselves
seriously enough to love their own flesh. Interestingly, here they join
hands with another set of intellectuals, who might at first seem to be
their opposites, the structuralists who understand conscious life through
its inscription by cultural codes, the new rationalists. The weak must
believe that they have been spoiled when the transcendent interpretations of civilization have been eclipsed. They seek the source of spolia-
tion in cultural history because there are no strong left to blame: the
weak who are entrenched in the systems of organized control trample
on the weak who are excluded from participation in those systems. Parasites disguised as predators lord it over parasites who are would-be
predators. The dogmatists of rationalism and empiricism both need to
be wrapped in a system: the first in order to excuse their impotence and
the second to explain it, but both to justify it.

It is here that the civil savage begins mapping postcivilized modernity. Postmodernist political, social, and cultural criticism is not a clarification of the contemporary human situation but a telling symptom of it. Its essence is an immoderation born of the feeling that one is missing out on the life that one should have, that existence is not the way that it is supposed to be, and that life has been organized in such a way that the exploiters are enjoying the inauthentic values of domination, possession, conspicuous consumption, and self-inflation, whereas the exploited are deprived of the genuine values of mutuality and sharing. And deep beneath that feeling of living the life that one should not have had to live is the horrified acknowledgment that one is compelled to care for oneself, that there is no unimpeachable ground for anyone to sacrifice for anyone else but only the voluntary decision to do so, and that such decisions are not made frequently enough to sustain a community. The truth of self-dependence is the revelation of postcivilized modernity, not the truth peculiar to postcivilized modernity, but the truth about human existence that becomes available and apparent in these times.

Life is apprehended neither as a stream of vital experience or will, nor as the inscription of codes by an alien culture, but as an objective structure with subjective reference, as the diversity of the flesh extended into the world and then springing back into the flesh, penetrating the psyche and superintended by the spirit. Culture, as Marshall McLuhan understood, is an extension, outerization, or exteriorization of the body and the psyche, and it can be no more. It cannot transcend its source in the sense of remaking it essentially though it can come to tyrannize it. That is, culture can never overcome the irremediable diversity and conflict within the flesh, within the psyche, and between psyche and flesh, spirit and flesh, and spirit and psyche. Indeed, when culture is demystified and becomes postcivilized, it becomes an objectification, a simulacrum, of Pauline inwardness, and then recoils into the self to exacerbate its original perplexity. Culture is the dismembered flesh, contrived imaginatively, which confronts its origin as a description and a judgment. Artificial intelligence is a judgment on the intellect, television a judgment on the expressive imagination, fast food a judgment on the taste buds, and bureaucracy a judgment on the will. Before culture had thoroughly encrusted primary nature, human existence could not know itself fully from without, as objective. Now we are trapped in a world of our own making, void of transcendence, and we are able to know who we are, without the assistance of an *imaginaire*, a utopia, a heaven, a repository of possibility suggesting an unrealized potentiality.

✧

The overpowering fact, which defines the new era of postcivilized modernity, is the externalization of culture and the objectification of the mind. In material culture this fact is evident in the deliverance of calculative reason to the computer, of transformative labor to robotics, of technical imagination to synthetics, and, most importantly, of perception and judgment to an environment of humanly produced objects that signify some sort of intention but that do not indicate any integral whole. In spiritual culture objectification is manifest in the materialization or substantialization of the expressive imagination into works of popular art such as television series, films, advertisements, and mass-circulation magazines. There is no longer any purchase for the speculative imagination to dream of a second reality beyond or beneath the obvious one, or of a future world that might be a home for human beings, a place where they might feel that they belonged.

The modern process has reached the stage at which it is absurd to hope for the revitalization of some received civilized tradition or for a new beginning, a revolutionary moment or an evolutionary consummation. Culture has become so dense and so disunified that the only changes that are reasonable to expect are alterations in specific complexes of cultural objects, modest reforms that will make some aspects of life less dangerous or malign, or further exacerbations of tensions, conflicts, and destructive tendencies. The success of the project of covering over nature with culture means that the possibilities of freedom toward the future have been narrowed because the materials on which imagination works have already been interpreted and reinterpreted many times over by other human beings. There is no wilderness into which a prophet or seer might wander to receive a fresh vision of being, for even a withdrawal into the wilderness of subjectivity reveals only the tracings of how others have treated and affected the self as transmitters of culture. We already live in the new jungle, forest, or desert; the cultural wasteland surrounds us and is carried with us into the new frontier of outer space. As the transcendence that supported civilization is effaced, the inhabitants of the postcivilized world retreat to the savagery familiar to the adherents of the God of Jerusalem, the idolatry of the old Adam.

The civil savage is the response to the emergence of an uncivil savagery, which flourishes in an environment shaped by the externalized mind, in which the individual imagination is tempted to abandon itself to transient self-gratification, to use ideas and beliefs as incitements to feeling good about the self momentarily. The pursuit of objective pleasures is the counterpoint (the subversive strategy) to the dominant theme (the official strategy) of substitute and subjective satisfaction.

Postcivilization is proximally and for the most part disclosed as a new polytheism, a crystallization of Emile Durkheim's collective consciousness into a circumstance of sensible objects that confront the self as simulations of itself. The animist spiritualized the world by endowing the objects of perceived nature with personality, casting a net of judgment over perception and only imperfectly concretizing that judgment through ritual. Precivilized life was nurtured by the *imaginaire*, which provided nature with intelligibility and, most importantly for the viewpoint of the monotheism of Jerusalem, offered the delusion, through the worship of graven images, that natural forces could be bent to human will. Postcivilization returns to animism, but now it is cultural and, therefore, void of magic and mystery. In place of the God-man is the celebrity, a celluloid image that can be invested with identification or cathexis, and then abandoned. In place of the man-God is the imaginary figure of advertising and propaganda, Ronald McDonald, Rambo, or the new socialist man. There are materialized presiding spirits of every place and time, which are treated with the same credulity and disdain as the precivilized savage treated fetishes; there are special sites for worship, sacred precincts, such as Disneyland, where totemic rituals are performed and the feats of technology are simulated technologically. The public environment is suffused with religion, so much so that the pervasive piety goes unacknowledged. That piety is terribly weak and cannot believe in itself, but it penetrates to the core of the uncivil savage, driving out all but devotion to the nice, the cute, and the spectacular.

The religion of postcivilized modernity is polytheistic, constituted by commercial, political, psychiatric, and more traditionally religious cults. There is room for every sort of belief and there are churches to cater to each one. Indeed, contemporary belief is most often syncretic, incorporating a number of fetishisms that are agglomerated to form a lifestyle. One may worship one's automobile, drawing self-inflating fantasies from it; and then one may commune with the TV, allowing the collectively contrived objective imagination to sweep one into a legitimate fantasy. None of this need be taken too seriously by the individual who indulges in it; it should not be felt deeply, just deeply enough to provoke the emotion of self-satisfaction. The civil savage does not dismiss the impact that a weak, disjointed, and all-encompassing piety, worship, and enthusiasm has on his uncivil fellows. He even entertains the idea that advertising and propaganda do not exist primarily to sell merchandise and secure power, but that commercial and political advantage are means to religious consummations: he imagines that one passes under the Golden Arches into a church, and that paying for the fast food is the same as dropping money into the collection plate, a contemporary communion. Postcivilized modernity has desublimated religion by creating concrete images for all human impulses and providing places and times for their worship, not for their genuine satisfaction, however, but only for their vicarious gratification through self-feeling. The old Adam at last dwells in his own world, not a new Eden or a new Jerusalem, but a temple of idols, the projections of his divided self.

The civil savage takes the dare of proclaiming that traditional civilization of eternal transcendence and modern civilization of transcendence toward the future are things of the past, and that human beings confront themselves today exactly as they always have essentially been but did not fully know themselves to be because they could look beyond themselves to something imaginary, something that had not yet been objectified or placed determinately into the world by human beings. The ubiquity of cultural animism (advertising and propaganda) in a society propelled by technology signals the triumph of the Pauline flesh, the will to pretend that being is tractable to whim, and the will to believe that pandering to weakness and desperately clinging to good feelings is the essence of existence. For the new polytheism everything must be invested with the indication that it is something more than it is, just as precivilized peoples endowed nature with the significance of myth. Yet the mythology of cultural animism is empty of significance: culture is not mysterious, it contains its meaning in the most mundane way, which is why it can never be mystified as a whole. The uncivil savage is the accomplice in collective schizophrenia.

The new polytheism expresses a society that has been irretrievably divided and is no longer the mass society that flourishes on abstract unification, as Gabriel Marcel had it, but is a society of separated masses, each with its appropriate cults that are manifested in lifestyles. The image of mass society was the last effort of modern civilization to imagine a social whole, albeit a negative one organized by greed, fear, and the quest for self-complacency. The ''mass man'' of Ortega desired to live in culture as though it were spontaneous, primary nature. According to Ortega, that wish was delusory because culture must be upheld by self-conscious effort and must ever be renewed by imagination disciplined to the requirements of mutating circumstance. The mass man was a spoiled child, a would-be aristocrat, who eschewed nobility and was indifferent to the authority of objectivity, a hermit in a state of radical dependence on others, a contradicted life bent on unmaking civilization. The civil savage declares that the mass man has triumphed so absolutely that he has been transformed into another type, the uncivil savage, a tribal being existing through fabricated solidarities. The tribalism of today is not something given, an ongoing milieu through which individuals pass, but a compensation for an imploded self mediated through crystallized collective representations. The mass man had a will, if only the will to put a stop to transcendence and to feed off the work of others, to democratize the rentier. The uncivil savage, in contrast, has no such will. Culture has become a second nature and, although Ortega was correct that it does not reproduce itself spontaneously but is only perpetuated through effort, it does not confront the individual as a project but as a dynamic complex of things. The uncivil savage does not, for the most part, demand anything from culture because he does not have sufficient distance from it to do that; rather he fills himself with culture and becomes a representative of it, a typeman. He allows culture to pervade him and then attempts to respond to it emotionally in the manner in which he anticipates that it desires him to feel. The uncivil savage tries to feel enthusiasm when that is suggested to him, or shock when that seems to be demanded, or self-righteous outrage when that is signaled. One is supposed to be enthusiastic about a trip to Disneyland or to the Super Bowl, so one tries to summon the proper feelings: one feels on cue. The precivilized savage did not, presumably, have to summon emotion from a void, but was carried through life by the reinforcement of primary groups. The new tribalism is mediated, forcing individuals, in their privacy, to create the environment of feeling that attaches them to culture. The externalization of the mind, the objectification of culture, halts at the feelings, which cannot be outerized. That failure is a curse for the postcivilized, the uncivil, savage, who wishes most deeply for the impossible, to be given good feelings.

The mass man felt good about himself; indeed, according to Ortega, that was his grave defect. The uncivil savage is in a condition prior to will, striving to feel good about himself and searching for signs from every quarter that he is ''okay.'' The externalized mind generates a profound loneliness based on a disuse and a consequent distrust of the personal imagination, which is the redeemer of solitude.

Here the civil savage's mapping of postcivilized modernity achieves its coordinates: the normal type today is the anhedonic who has the self-referential project of feeling good about himself. He can succeed in gaining transient feelings of self-worth and self-satisfaction by feeling the way that he thinks he is supposed to feel in response to the culture that penetrates him. Now I understand why I declare myself to be the civil savage. There is a clear choice for those who can conceive of it between concentrating on one's own sense of vitality, the last bit of primary nature left, and trying to make one's own being into a proper sensorium for ever-changing cultural complexes. Personal imagination can no longer be the redeemer of solitude: the final reason for privacy is to feel one's own life and from that basis to work one's way back into the world to appropriate culture for pleasure and not to contrive the emotions that it is supposed to generate. Thus, I stake my life on irony instead of credulity, on devotion rather than disdain. I seize the fetishes and extract from them their vitalizing potential, even if that potential be only a healthy disgust or the laughter of the black humorist: let me listen to the laugh tracks of TV situation comedies not to stimulate my own laughter but to sensitize me to the specificity of the second nature. Let me deconstruct culture, not as an exercise but as a lifestrategy. I shall at least know the new wilderness intimately and I shall respond to it through my own vitality. Does this seem to be too modest a proposal? It will only appear to be so to someone who believes that will, intelligence, and imagination can still be unified collectively to provide the basis for a community. Otherwise the tolerance of inward life and attentiveness to its responses to culture, apart from prejudgments, is the way to living well and to taking pleasure.

The uncivil savage is alienated from inward vitality, and he experiences feeling as a function of the reception of culture. The society of masses is the structure through which selves who have been voided of imagination and whose will has been alienated to a technological apparatus stabilize their self-feeling. Social preference and social condition have been projected by the media of the externalized imagination into lifestyles that the appropriate individuals can take up as definitive of the self. There is, for example, a ''yuppie'' mass, a black underclass, an Evangelical mass, a gay mass, and a feminist mass, each exclusive of the others and each committed to fortifying a type of life based on particular preferences and proper emotions. Within these masses are networks of ''support groups'' that reinforce self-feeling by foreclosing doubt and irony, and whipping up earnestness and enthusiasm. The characteristic relation of the society of masses is an eviscerated form of therapy in which the partners unburden themselves of their grievances and then assure one another that they should feel good about themselves. Such an assurance is, it seems, the greatest gift that can be offered by one individual to another in postcivilized modernity: there is nothing wrong with you, you haven't been inadequate, it wasn't your fault. Yet, beneath that judgment, let me dare to say, is a deeper absolution: you are forgiven for not having been able to enjoy yourself, for not finding life worth living; you are permitted, nay encouraged, to believe that you have been crippled, that you have missed out on what you should have had, that your life is not what a "real" life should be. Modernity has worked beyond Nietzsche's "last man" to the type who craves being justified for having failed without having tried or, even more pathetically, for having been so weak as to have tried only according to the requirements of the culture that have been directed to him. This is the inwardness of the new polytheist: worship of the fetish is the response to having given up on delight or to having never grasped its possibility. Lifestyle and therapy are the compensations for devitalization: if I do not have my own pleasure I should try to be pleased with what I am supposed to have.

Politics was, in modern civilization, active reflection on the public situation; that is, a deliberate process of creating and maintaining sufficient order among contending interests to permit them to coexist with one another without decline into civil warfare. The modern project of political coordination presupposes a society that is coherent enough to be organized, in which the groups composing it share some consensus on the desirability of living together or, lacking that, in which some groups are powerful enough to impose their plans for living on the others. It is just such social coherence, however, that has been lost in the society of masses and, along with it, any incentives for individuals to commit themselves to solidarity with those with whom they share a common context of space and time. Yet, so long as collective life is to be perpetuated, especially in a technological matrix that forces people into material interdependence, some apparatus must exist to enforce the conditions for physical security.

The contemporary state is the political legacy of modern civilization, constituting an elaborate bureaucratic and decisional mechanism for encouraging and restricting more primary activities. The modern civilized state was based on the self-conscious limitation of coercive enforcement according to constitutional arrangements and a public opinion supporting them. The tyranny of organized sectoral groups was checked most importantly by guarantees of individual rights, which allowed people to reject received bonds and to forge new ones, loosening particular loyalties and opening up mobility. The emergence of totalitarianism in the twentieth century has shown, perhaps more starkly than any other historical development, the failure of modern civilization, its public deconstruction. The political analogue of modern civilization's formula of personal transcendence over given social ties through individual adherence to a rational idea or ideal is the constitutional protection of rights, which is annulled by totalitarianism, leaving, as Max Weber understood before the event, only a mechanical instrument of control that is capable of being utilized to apply an indefinite range of formulae for living. The externalization of the political mind, the decisional will, preceded the externalization of the imagination and has been familiar for more than a half century. The citizen, even in those states retaining constitutional procedures, has become a constituent and a receptor of rewards and punishments programmed by a hierarchy.

The early instances of totalitarianism, Bolshevism, fascism, and Nazism, were transitional forms between modern civilization and postcivilized modernity, each one attempting to substitute for individual liberty some substantive ideal of common life and an image of personality to accord with it. Ideological politics was an effort to reverse the process of demystification and to institute, as Ernst Cassirer noted, a new tribalism. Yet in the society of masses mystification has become too dispersed, disjointed, and pervasive to be coordinated into an overarching myth of the state. A pluralization and volatilization of tribes have occurred and the state has returned to what it was for Hobbes, a pure security apparatus that surely fosters a cult but cannot contain, much less synthesize, the new polytheism. Contrary to current popular myth, totalitarianism is currently in the process of being fulfilled throughout the industrialized world, but not in a romantic form: the political formula of postcivilized modernity is liberal fascism. The civil savage does not take that oxymoron lightly. The kind of state that expresses a self whose ego has been weakened to the point that the purpose of life is not to live well but to feel good enough about the self to want to live at all, is one that promises to provide safety above any other good, which promotes the freedom that cancels liberty, the freedom from risk. Modern civilization's protection of initiative has ceded to postcivilized modernity's will to save the very skin that it degrades and dishonors.

Why should I call the desperate quest for security through the state the "fascist" expression or possibility of liberalism? What is liberal about it? Let me reiterate the paradox: the uncivil savage seeks most deeply from the state the freedom from risk and maybe not only that but also the freedom from having to experience anything that will make him feel uncomfortable about himself. The wish not to have to suffer from living, not to have to tolerate the inherent weaknesses of the flesh, is the bad conscience of liberalism come to overt expression in crusades against drugs, drunk driving, cigarette smoking, unhealthy diets, and environmental pollution. Who will complain about these crusades, even if they are ineffective and require incessant monitoring and "invasions of privacy"? In every bid for security and safety there is an all-too-human desire to eliminate adversity. There is a corrosive irony in post-civilized politics: the externalization of all of the weaknesses of the flesh in an all-embracing second nature is attended by a drive to avoid the consequences of those weaknesses. If every negative freedom implies some positive state that is sought, the yearning for a safety state involves perhaps a longing for religious freedom, the freedom to watch television and go to Disneyland, the freedom to be the new polytheist dwelling within the externalized imagination, always freedom as schizophrenic detachment, living from the flesh into projected fantasy.

Liberal fascism and postcivilized modernity as a whole is a waiting game. The transitional totalitarianisms of the first half of the twentieth century projected ideals of a new human being: the Aryan blond beast, the new socialist man, and that tepid American counterpart, the well-adjusted personality. That era of heroism, which found its purest expression in Nietzsche's overman, has now concluded. Rather than any positive ideal of individual or collective overcoming, postcivilized modernity projects as its cultural horizon and its essential meaning, the bionic man, who is the simulacrum of the flesh, freed by genetic engineering, controlled environments, organ transplantation, and finally by a complete laboratory synthesis from the common complaints of the old Adam. Thus, the desperate preoccupation with the flesh in order to free the spirit to entertain contrived collective fantasy is but the prelude to the supersession of the flesh. Has there ever been as deep a hatred of human beings for themselves, for their own lives? All of the unconscious ironies of our times are intelligible so long as one understands the wisdom of the classical civilizations about the condition of the individual who has no contact with transcendence and who does not live by the laws formulated in terms of contact with some transcendent experience. The uncivil savage is the idol worshipper who was routed by

Abraham. Only now the idol is dynamic and efficacious, a kind of failed
Moloch.

⌁

Ortega did not foresee that his self-satisfied mass man was only a
transitional type who would become, as the "barbarism of specialization" worked its way into every corner of life, the uncivil savage who
is radically dissatisfied with the self, but who is not impelled by that
dissatisfaction to overcome himself in the service of a self-given standard, and who instead seeks to become mass or to be self-satisfied. The
basis of this further complication of modern consciousness is the creation of a cultural environment that overwhelms the human flesh and
psyche and that crushes the spirit, forcing the individual to seek security
in collectively produced fantasy. The mass man identified himself with
the achievements of modern civilization, trusted that they would be
maintained and expanded, and rebelled only against participating in the
strenuous effort required to perpetuate them. The spoiled child believed
that he had parents, protectors who would continue to provide for him
and permit him to be irresponsible.

That is, the mass man still shared in the dream of modern civilization
and had not yet experienced its eclipse; his self-satisfaction was sustained by a margin of hope, a shred of subjective imagination mediating
between present and future. Culture had not yet been fully externalized
and could still be felt as pregnant with possibilities, a potential plenitude, as Ortega had it. Today, in contrast, the mass man's successor
feels a profound distrust of culture and senses that there are no protectors. The dehumanization of culture signals an age in which individuals
feel constitutively inadequate to human creation. The new polytheism
expresses a condition in which human beings are surrounded with
works of imagination that confront them with representations of what
they can never experience and enjoy. In high technology they confront
powers that they can never hope to understand, much less to master.
Television provides an agglomeration of defective yet unattainable be-
atific visions and the computer offers a simulacrum of a higher will,
guided by artificial intelligence that is indifferent to joy and suffering.
The mass man rebelled against civilization and still desired, in an exercise of bad faith, to enjoy its fruits. The uncivil savage worships culture,
just as human beings have always worshipped that upon which they
radically depend and that they cannot control. Since the culture that

overmasters them is irremediably disunified, they worship it in a precivilized way, as a series of fetishes, hoping that adjusting their feelings to it will render it benign. Yet this whole desperate waiting game is contrived from the beginning because the object of worship must at some moments be grasped, if only dimly, as merely another human product, void of mystery, of transcendent possibility. Postcivilized modernity means the worship of idol as idol.

The civil savage does not morally reprove his uncivil fellows for their fetishism, which he understands as the human-all-too-human response to the terribly difficult task of living in a world shot through with adversity. He must even feel compassion for the growing numbers of individuals whose most profound need is to feel good about themselves because they feel their inadequacy to the humanized world so keenly and cannot tolerate their self-judgment. Ortega and the other theorists of mass society, such as Marcel, Karl Jaspers, and the members of the Frankfurt school, could deliver moral criticism because they believed that the crisis of modern civilization was precipitated by a failure of will. Now the crisis has passed and it becomes clear that the cause of the failure of civilization was objective, that is, was the very process of objectification that stripped culture of any unifying intention and deprived it of any indication of a reference beyond itself. The *imaginaire* has materialized and is, therefore, as stubbornly finite as the flesh. It is here and there to be seized upon for exactly what it yields through itself and through individual wit: since he is less than its appropriator, the uncivil savage craves having it be more than himself, having it function as the fetishes of the precivilized savage and the symbols of transcendence of the civilized man did. The religious impulse permeates postcivilized modernity.

In place of moral criticism, the civil savage substitutes a mapping of the environment, which he undertakes in order to discover the points at which connections with the world and others can be made that are productive of objective and genuine pleasures. He experiences an objectless gratitude for those stretches of his life that are marked by surplus vitality, keen sensibility, and the disposition to enjoy that which is other to himself; he seeks to open up more of those stretches by fitting himself to tolerate abuse and to cherish good. He is different from the uncivil savage because he has brought the ironies of postcivilized modernity to self-consciousness and has concluded that moments of real connection that can be wrenched from an environment of contrived fantasy are better than submission to that fantasy. That conclusion is the basis of a life strategy that can only be offered to others as an invitation, not as an imperative.

There are essentially three life-strategies available in postcivilized modernity. The one that is most tempting is to be the new polytheist who embraces the waiting game and descends into fetishism. Indeed, it is so tempting that it is usually embraced unconsciously. The second option is to live in the nostalgic reminiscence of civilization, pretending that it might be restored and, perhaps, gaining a sense of self-righteous superiority and self-importance from the pretense. Obviously that is just another way of feeling good about oneself, and of hiding in a stance of superiority or cultural elitism. The third alternative, the civil savage's, is to delight in the pleasures of the world and to cherish the objects that, and the people who, provide them.

The civil savage is the old Adam expelled from the garden for the second time, this time from the garden of civilization into the wilderness of culture. As the civil savage, I have no law to guide me but possess only my own wits as I pick through the ruins of civilization and bring the treasures that I discover into the anhedonic culture of subjective and substitute pleasures. I am a partisan of the flesh and the psyche against the bionic man and the fabricated self-image. I pit my own vitality against the impulse to inflate self-feeling and dispose myself to love what is favorable in the world instead of entertaining the *imaginaire*. In order to come to myself I have had to surrender only the wish and the hope that there is some possibility or potentiality of human nature beyond what has already been discovered about it, some essential or saving possibility or potentiality. Such surrender is no sacrifice for me, but is instead an opportunity to enjoy what is enjoyable thoroughly and without pretense or contrivance for the first time, perhaps for the first time in history.

⬦

Notes

Chapter 1. Civilization
   1. I am indebted to Chen-te Yang for this translation.

Chapter 2. Defensive Life
   1. David Swenson, ''Objective Uncertainty and Human Faith,'' *Philosophical Review* 37 (September 1928):433–59.

Index

.

About the Author

Michael A. Weinstein is Professor of Political Science at Purdue University in West Lafayette, Indiana. He is the author of 21 books and more than 100 articles in the fields of political theory, philosophy, sociological theory, political science, cultural theory, and literary and photography criticism. Specializing in twentieth-century discourse, especially philosophy of life, conduct, and culture, Weinstein has contributed to the literatures of existentialism, pragmatism, and post-modernism. He has held Guggenheim and Rockefeller Foundation fellowships, is the photography critic for *New City* in Chicago, and performs rap songs. Weinstein's recent books in postmodern theory are *Data Trash* (with Arthur Kroker) (1994) and *Postmodern(ized) Simmel* (with Deena Weinstein) (1993).